ALGEBRAIC SPECIFICATION OF COMMUNICATION PROTOCOLS

**Cambridge Tracts in Theoretical
Computer Science**

Managing Editor   Professor C.J. van Rijsbergen,
Department of Computing Science, University of Glasgow

Titles in the series

ALGEBRAIC SPECIFICATION OF COMMUNICATION PROTOCOLS

Edited by

S. Mauw
Eindhoven University of Technology

G.J. Veltink
ISYTEC, Bremen

CAMBRIDGE
UNIVERSITY PRESS

CAMBRIDGE UNIVERSITY PRESS
Cambridge, New York, Melbourne, Madrid, Cape Town, Singapore, São Paulo, Delhi

Cambridge University Press
The Edinburgh Building, Cambridge CB2 8RU, UK

Published in the United States of America by Cambridge University Press, New York

www.cambridge.org
Information on this title: www.cambridge.org/9780521418836

First published 1993
This digitally printed version 2008

A catalogue record for this publication is available from the British Library

ISBN 978-0-521-41883-6 hardback
ISBN 978-0-521-08812-1 paperback

CONTENTS

   J.J. van Wamel

PREFACE

The specifications in this book are the result of a number of case studies performed by researchers from the Programming Research Group at the University of Amsterdam. The primary goal was to study the use of the techniques developed by the Programming Research Group for the specification of real-life protocols. From the pool of available case studies we made a selection that focuses on communication protocols, which we present in an order well suited for use in education. We hope that this book provides a first step towards a methodology for the design of communication protocols using PSF.

The following people have contributed to this book: Jacob Brunekreef, Henrik Jacobsson[1], Sjouke Mauw[2], Gert Veltink[3] and Jos van Wamel.

Other people have helped in initiating and creating this book. The editors would like to express their gratitude for their help in various ways to Jan Bergstra, Jacob Brunekreef, Bob Diertens, Casper Dik, Hans Kamps, Hans Mulder and Jos van Wamel.

December 1992
S.M./G.J.V.

---

[1] current affiliation Oracle Netherlands

[2] current affiliation Eindhoven University of Technology,
e-mail: sjouke@win.tue.nl

[3] current affiliation Institute for Applied System Technology Bremen,
e-mail: veltink@isytec.uucp

CHAPTER 1
INTRODUCTION

S. MAUW & G.J. VELTINK

1.1 AIM AND SCOPE

An important reason why formal description techniques are not appreciated as widely as wished by the developers of such techniques, is that people who actually design and implement software have relatively little knowledge of formal methods. The acceptance of formal techniques not only depends on the existence of techniques that are easy to understand and easy to use, but also on the training of potential users. This implies that there is a need for text books and case-studies. We think that a collection of formal specifications in a restricted area of application may help to get a better understanding of the use of formal techniques. Although the method we use is well suited for formal verification, we concentrate on the act of specification. A first requirement for a formal correctness proof is a formal specification.

We restrict ourselves in this book to a collection of specifications concerning one application area, the field of communication protocols. Although this seems to be an area with a relatively high acceptance of formal techniques, most of the protocols that are actually in use are specified in natural language, if ever specified otherwise than by the actual implementation. Even well-known and accepted standards, such as the token ring protocol, do not have a rigorous formal definition. Informal specifications in this area may lead to misinterpretations and, thus, to different implementations that will not be able to work together. Formal techniques are especially needed for communication protocol design, since these protocols describe distributed systems which have a high degree of non-determinism. This implies

1

that errors are not easily detected and hard to reproduce, which makes traditional testing techniques too unreliable for validation purposes.

The protocols described in this book cover a wide range. We start with the description of simple point-to-point protocols, such as the Alternating Bit Protocol, which have been specified and verified many times with a variety of formal techniques. The more complex protocols in this book are used in practice and some of them have never been subject of formal specification and verification before.

The main aim of this book is to provide the reader with a collection of protocol descriptions which illustrates how to use algebraic specification techniques, be it in the field of communication protocols or in a related area. Furthermore, we wish to give insight in the design and operation of communication protocols. The specifications in this book have a level of abstraction that is appropriate for a clear understanding of the protocols without having to deal with implementation details.

Although based on a formal theory of concurrent processes, this book can be understood without previous knowledge of process algebras. We think that beginners as well as professionals in the field of communication protocols will benefit from studying the protocol descriptions provided. The sections on simple protocols are tutorial, whereas the more complex protocols are topics of current research and are being used in modern networks.

1.2   FORMAL METHODS

In academia it is generally recognized that formal methods are a useful technique for software design. The main advantage of the use of formal techniques is that a formal specification is a mathematical object which has an unambiguous meaning, therefore mathematical methods may be used to analyse these specifications, such as formal verification of the correctness and completeness of a specification.

Formal methods play a vital rôle, especially in the field of protocol standardization. Standards are needed for providing connectivity among systems. Adhering to a formal specification guarantees that system components from different manufacturers can be interchanged easily. A formal specification can be used to derive test cases automatically, in order to check whether a particular implementation behaves as expected. If the implementation language is a formal language as well, it even makes it possible to verify formally that an implementation satisfies a given specification.

For most formal techniques, software tools have been developed that aid in analyzing a given specification. Apart from syntax-checking and type-checking, most software environments for formal methods also provide a means for rapid prototyping. Even automatic generation of an implementation is sometimes possible. Other tools can generate test sequences that can be used for conformance testing, which is an important validation activity in the construction of software.

A great variety of formal specification techniques exist, some of which are general purpose (such as Z, VDM or COLD), while others are generally used in a specific domain of application (such as LOTOS, SDL and PSF). The mathematical theories on which these languages are based range from set theory and temporal logic to lambda-calculus and process algebra.

Formal methods have been applied in the design of a great number of systems. Many protocols have been specified and verified formally. Some protocol standards are even defined by means of a formal method.

The specifications in this book are written in the language PSF (Process Specification Formalism). This is a formal specification language based on the Algebra of Communicating Processes (ACP). PSF can be seen as a concrete representation for the process theory ACP. Furthermore, PSF supports the use of abstract data types and has special features for modularization and parameterization of specifications.

ACP is a theory for the specification and verification of concurrent systems. It can be viewed as a generalization of other theories for concurrency such as CCS and CSP. An ACP specification consists of a collection of algebraic process definitions and verification is done by algebraic manipulation of these processes. Its semantics are relatively simple and it can be extended easily with special features such as real time and interrupts. ACP has been applied in the specification and verification of many concurrent systems.

In this book we advocate the use of algebraic techniques for protocol specification. However, we regard the PSF language as one of the many ways to obtain formal protocol specifications and do not claim that it is the specification language best suited for communication protocols in general.

1.3 COMPUTER NETWORKS

The way in which people interact with computers has changed significantly since their introduction. In the early days only one user could be working with a computer at a time. The introduction of so-called *time-sharing* systems made it possible for computers to be used by a number of users at the same time. Nowadays, with decreasing prices of computer hardware, mainframes are being more and more replaced by clusters of smaller machines connected by a *network*. An important reason for this is that the price/performance ratio of a personal computer is much better than that of a mainframe.

A second reason for using networks, is that they allow one to construct systems that share resources like *file servers* and *printers*. Such systems can also achieve an increased reliability by offering duplicated services. If one computer or peripheral device is out of order, other machines can take over its tasks.

The final reason for using computer networks, is that they make it possible to connect computer systems that are spread out geographically. A company with branches all over the world that each have their local computer systems can access information about all different branches through a network that connects the local systems.

1.3.1   LANS & WANS

There are two important classes of networks. A Local Area Network (LAN) is used when the distances between the computers are not too large. A typical example is a network that connects the computers in one building. Each user has his own computer and all users share output devices and storage devices using the LAN.

A Wide Area Network (WAN) is used when the distance between two computers is larger, for example to establish a connection between different cities. An example of a world-wide WAN is *USENET*. One of the services offered by this network is *electronic mail*, which enables people all around the world to exchange messages.

1.3.2   NETWORK STRUCTURE

A network consists of a collection of computers, called *hosts*, and a *subnet* that connects the hosts. The subnet consists of *transmission lines*, the medium through which the data is transported, and special dedicated processors IMPs (Interface Message Processor) which connect two or more communication channels.

There are two important designs for the subnet. The first design uses a so-called *point-to-point* subnet. All IMPs are connected by wires or telephone lines. IMPs that are directly connected can communicate with each other. However, two IMPs that are not directly connected must use one or more intermediate IMPs to communicate. Messages are sent to an intermediate IMP that stores them and waits until the channel to the next IMP is free and sends the message further. Most WANs are implemented using point-to-point subnets.

The second communication architecture, which is mainly used in LANs, uses a mechanism called *broadcasting*. Whenever a message is sent by one machine, all other machines connected to the subnet receive this message. The message contains an address, which indicates for which machine the message was intended. The receiving stations that do not have a matching address, simply discard the message.

1.3.3   OSI REFERENCE MODEL

In the previous section we discussed how computers can be connected on the physical level. Having such a connection does not automatically imply that two computers can *understand* each other. It might well be the case that both computers use a different way of representing information. To make sure that they can communicate they have to adhere to certain agreements of how to exchange data. Such an agreement is called a *protocol*.

In the early days of networks, each manufacturer used his own protocols. Such an approach makes it difficult to connect systems of different manufacturers. To overcome such problems the ISO (International Standards Organization) has made a proposal for an international standard for networking. This standard is called the ISO OSI (Open Systems Interconnection) Reference Model.

The OSI model is divided into seven layers, as shown in Figure 1.1. One important reason for dividing the network into layers is to reduce the design complexity of a network system. Each layer has its own specific task and offers services to a higher layer, based on the services offered by a lower layer. In this way a layer is shielded from the *implementation details* of lower layers.

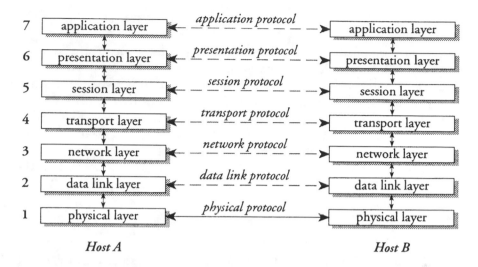

Figure 1.1   The ISO OSI Reference Model

A layer on level *n* on one computer communicates with the layer on level *n* on another computer. The set of rules for communication that they adhere to is called the *protocol* of layer *n*. The processes in the same layer, in two different computers that communicate with each other, are called *peer* processes.

There is no direct transmission of data from layer *n* on one machine to layer *n* on the other machine. Instead, data is sent to the layer immediately below, until the physical layer is reached. The physical layer forms the only actual connection between two computers. All other layers are in fact different levels of abstraction of communication.

The seven layers are roughly divided into two groups, levels 1 to 4 are called the *communication layers* and we refer to the levels 5 to 7 as *application layers*. The lower layers take care of the exchange of information between two computers. The upper layers contain, among others, encryption and decryption techniques, transformations between different methods of character representation such as ASCII and EBCDIC, and routines for transferring a file from one file system to another. Only the communication layers of the OSI model will be of interest for the topics treated in this book, so we will briefly describe their functions.

The *physical layer* is dedicated to the transmission of bits over a physical communication channel. In this layer there are standards that describe how the different bit values 0 and 1 must be represented.

The transmission of data on the physical level can be distorted in many ways, because data often has to travel a long way through physically unreliable channels, such as the atmosphere and telephone wires. It is the responsibility of the *data link layer* to transform this unreliable connection into an error-free communication channel for the higher layers.

The main task of the *network layer* is to determine the route by which data has to travel through the network. If data has to travel from one network to another, it is also the responsibility of the network layer to offer services that enable this coupling of networks.

It is the responsibility of the *transport layer* to decide how a *transport connection*, needed by the higher layers, is mapped onto the available *network connections*. If two hosts are connected by more than one network connection, the transport layer can decide to split the data and send it along the different network connections to achieve better performance. This technique is called *downward multiplexing*. On the other hand it is possible that the upper layers need more transport connections than available network connections. In this case the transport layer can decide to merge the data of several transport connections, so that they can be transported over fewer network connections. This technique is called *upward multiplexing*.

1.3.4   TERMINOLOGY

The protocols that are described in this book, are mainly situated in the data link layer. We recall that the main task of this layer is to offer the network layer an error-free communication channel. In this section we will introduce the terminology used in the specifications of the protocols from the data link layer.

The specifications deal with the transmission of data from a *sender* to a *receiver*, via a *channel*. There are three possibilities of data transfer along a channel with respect to the direction of the data.

- *simplex*: data can be transported in only one direction
- *half-duplex*: data can be transported in both directions but only in one direction at a time
- *full-duplex*: data can be transported in both directions at the same time

To be able to detect transmission errors that may occur in the physical layer, the data stream is augmented with extra information also called a *checksum*. The method normally used to calculate this checksum is the Cyclic Redundancy Code (CRC). The receiver verifies the checksum of the incoming data and if this verification fails it raises a *checksum error* to indicate that something went wrong. One possible action then is to ask the sender to retransmit the garbled data.

In the PSF specifications it is required that a communication channel is *fair*. This means that a channel does not produce an infinite stream of garbled data, but that it will sooner or later transmit a datum correctly.

1.4   OVERVIEW

This book contains seven chapters, most of which can be read and understood independently. A prerequisite for understanding Chapters 3 to 7 is knowledge of the PSF language, which is explained in Chapter 2. All specifications in this book are analyzed with the checking and simulation tools from the PSF-Toolkit. Knowledge of the PSF-Toolkit, which is also described in Chapter 2, is not necessary for understanding the specifications.

Chapters 3 and 4 are concerned with point-to-point protocols, that is, protocols which communicate information from one fixed location to another (and possibly back) using an unreliable channel. It is advisable to read Chapter 3 before Chapter 4. Chapter 3 contains a specification of three simple protocols for simplex communication. These are the alternating bit protocol (ABP), a protocol with positive acknowledgement and retransmissions (PAR), and the concurrent alternating bit protocol (CABP). They differ in the sense that PAR and CABP can handle "lossy" channels, while ABP can only correct mutilated messages. In the PAR protocol a timer is used to overcome lost messages, while in the CABP this is solved by sending a continuous stream of messages.

Chapter 4 contains three more-evolved point-to-point protocols from the class of sliding window protocols. These protocols are full-duplex. The simplest is the one-bit protocol, which has a sending window and a receiving window of size 1. Such a window is a buffer which contains messages that are not yet acknowledged. A more efficient protocol is the "pipelining with go back N" protocol, which has a sending window size greater than 1. A still more efficient protocol is the "nonsequential receive with selective repeat" protocol which also has a receiving window greater than 1.

Chapter 5 contains a protocol for communication in a distributed operating system; the Amoeba Transaction protocol. It is used in the Amoeba distributed operating system for information exchange between two processes.

Chapters 6 and 7 contain protocols for Local Area Networks. A simple token ring protocol and a simple ethernet protocol are specified in Chapter 6. The simple token ring protocol can be used in a network with a ring architecture. The simple ethernet protocol is a CSMA/CD (Carrier Sense Multiple Access with Collision Detection) protocol, which is used on a bus architecture.

A specification of a token ring protocol based on the formal IEEE standard (IEEE 8802/4) is given in Chapter 7.

1.5 BIBLIOGRAPHICAL NOTES

There are two books that are strongly related to this book: *Process Algebra* ([BW90]) and *Applications of Process Algebra* ([Bae90]). We consider [BW90] as a basic text on process algebra theory and [Bae90] as an example of the application of this theory, especially in the sense of correctness verification. In our view, this collection of protocol specifications demonstrating the practical use of process algebra will link up nicely with the two aforementioned books.

This book is completely self-contained, in the sense that it can be read without previous knowledge of the process theory explained in [BW90]. Nevertheless we expect that this book will stimulate readers to take an interest in the theoretical backgrounds of concurrency theory. One can take full advantage of the formal method used in this book by studying both the mathematical background from [BW90] and the verification examples of [Bae90].

The PSF language is defined in [MV90]. Other formal methods are described in [FJ92], [VDM88], [SDL84] and [ISO89]. The theory ACP was developed by Bergstra and Klop [BK84]. CCS and CSP are other theories for the specification of concurrent systems. They are described in [Mil89] and [Hoa85].

There are a number of other examples of the use of PSF and ACP concerning the specification of communication protocols. These are, amongst others [MW89], [Mau90], [MM90] and [VW92].

A comprehensive introduction to the OSI model is [HS88]. More general books on computer networks are [Tan89] and [Sch87].

CHAPTER 2
ALGEBRAIC SPECIFICATIONS IN PSF

G.J. VELTINK

2.1 INTRODUCTION

In this chapter we will focus on the specification language used throughout this book: PSF (Process Specification Formalism). We will discuss the mathematical origins of PSF as well as its syntax and semantics. The language itself will be clarified by using a running example, which gets more complicated as new language features are introduced. Apart from giving specifications in PSF we will also describe the implementations that make up the so-called PSF-Toolkit, such as the *term rewriting system* and the *simulator*.

The PSF-Toolkit also embodies a collection of frequently used specifications in the form of the PSF standard library. In this chapter we will explain which modules are part of the library and how they can be used. A full listing of the relevant modules from the PSF standard library can be found in Appendix A.

2.2 ACP

Before we turn our attention to PSF, we will give some information on ACP (Algebra of Communicating Processes). ACP is the theoretical foundation for the process part of PSF, and deserves some explanation as such.

The development of ACP was started in 1982 by J.A. Bergstra and J.W. Klop, at the Centre for Mathematics and Computer Science in Amsterdam. Compared with other concurrency theories like CCS, CSP and Petri Nets, ACP is most closely allied to CCS. The main difference between ACP and the other approaches is the way in which the semantics is treated.

Most formalisms, like CCS, CSP and Petri Nets are based on one specific model of concurrency. ACP, however, is a theory based on algebraic methods[†]. The theory is defined by a set of axioms. The collection of possible models of this set of axioms contains most of the models for concurrency that have been proposed. By extending or restricting this set of axioms and by adding new operators, one can change the collection of possible models. This is a more general approach than the one which focuses on a single model. In many cases an algebraic approach towards verification has advantages over the model based approach.

2.3 THE HISTORY OF PSF

Several small tools for ACP were constructed between 1982 and 1986, but the lack of a unifying framework led to many inconsistencies between these tools. In the Autumn of 1987 the PAT (Process Algebra Tools) project was started. This project aimed at constructing an integrated environment of computer tools for studying concurrent systems, especially in the setting of ACP.

The first step towards this goal was the definition of PSF, a computer readable language to specify ACP processes. Although ACP uses data types in an informal way, it was felt that PSF should incorporate data types on a more formal basis. The language definition of PSF was completed in the Spring of 1988.

The definition of data types and modularization concepts in PSF is based on the algebraic specification language ASF (Algebraic Specification Language). The language ASF was developed at the Centre for Mathematics and Computer Science in Amsterdam.

The relation between ACP, ASF and PSF is given by Figure 2.1. The three blocks represent the *building blocks* from which PSF has been constructed.

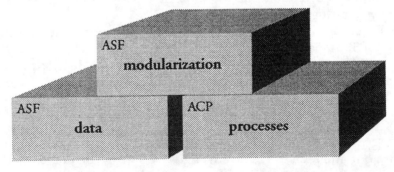

Figure 2.1   The constituent parts of PSF

[†] We notice that in this text book series two volumes on process algebra in the style of ACP have already appeared. One book describing the mathematical foundations of ACP and one collected volume describing different applications of ACP.

After the PSF language had been defined, work on the tools started. This resulted in a compiler for PSF and several tools such as a simulator and a term rewriter. A detailed description of this still expanding set of tools is contained in this chapter.

2.4 PSF: Syntax and Semantics

In this section we will focus on the syntax and semantics of PSF. We will explain the elements of the language by specifying a simple protocol that gradually becomes more complicated as new language constructs are used. After a language construct has been introduced in an example, we will discuss its usage, general appearance and semantics. The full grammar of PSF can be found in Appendix B.

2.4.1 Basic Operators

PSF specifications deal with the description of the activity of processes, and the interaction between different processes. The term *process* in this context must be interpreted in a broad sense. It can range from the behaviour of a drinks dispenser and production processes in a factory to the behaviour of human beings.

The basic manifestation of activity in PSF is represented by an *atomic action*. In this book the terms atomic action, as well as *atom* and *action* will be used. Each atomic action has a name or *label* and whenever an atomic action with name a is active, we say that a happens.

Processes in PSF are defined in terms of *process expressions*. The atomic action is the basic process expression. Complex process behaviour in PSF is expressed by combining process expressions in different ways using additional *operators*. In PSF there are for instance operators that tell whether two process expressions are to be executed in succession, simultaneously or that a choice has to be made between either one of them.

2.4.1.1 Action Relations

To attach *semantics* or meaning to the operators, we describe their behaviour by means of a mathematical notation called *action relations*. For each atomic action a we define a binary relation and a unary relation on process expressions. The notation of the two relations is given below. The dots represent process expressions.

$$\bullet \xrightarrow{a} \bullet \qquad \bullet \xrightarrow{a} \sqrt{}$$

Table 2.1   Action relations

When x and y are variables for process expressions, the notation $x \xrightarrow{a} y$ expresses the fact that x can evolve into y by executing the atomic action a. The notation for the unary relation, $x \xrightarrow{a} \sqrt{}$, is used to express that x, after having executed atomic action a, can reach a state in which it has terminated successfully. The $\sqrt{}$ symbol (tick) indicates successful termination of a process.

The simplest action relation states that a process expression consisting of a single atomic action a, can terminate successfully by executing this atomic action a. This action rule is given by:

$$a \xrightarrow{a} \sqrt{}$$

Table 2.2   Action relation for atomic action

2.4.1.2 The Example

The running example that we will use is an abstraction of the protocol specifications to follow. Only the basic elements of a specification of a protocol are kept. The example describes, like most protocol specifications, a sender and receiver pair that are connected to each other by a channel. The goal is to transmit data from the sender to the receiver via the channel.

The graphical representation of the example is given below. The three different processes are represented by boxes. The dots in the boxes represent the atomic actions that a process is able to perform. The interaction between the different components is not modelled.

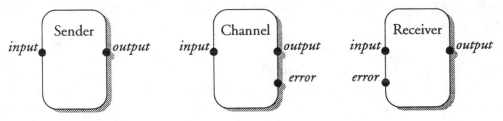

Figure 2.2   Graphical representation of the components of the running example

2.4.1.3 Identifier Names, Lexical Conventions

Entities in a PSF specification are referred to by a name. These names or *identifiers* must meet some lexical requirements. The *identifier character set* of PSF consists of all lower case characters $(a, b, ..., z)$, all upper case characters $(A, B, ..., Z)$, all digits $(0, 1, ..., 9)$ and the special symbols *single quote* (') and *hyphen* (-). A valid identifier in PSF is a string starting with a lower case or upper case character, followed by zero or more characters from the identifier character set.

In this book we will print all keywords in PSF specifications in bold face. This is not part of the lexical conventions of PSF, but only serves to increase the legibility of the specifications.

2.4.1.4 Comments

Comments in PSF are introduced by two consecutive hyphens (--). Comments are closed by another pair of hyphens or by the *newline* character, whichever one comes first. Within the text of the comment, characters from the complete character set of the host computer can be used, with the exception of the above-mentioned newline and pair of hyphens.

2.4.1.5 Atoms & Processes

The first PSF specification, representing the sender from Figure 2.2, is given below:

```
process module Sender
begin

   atoms
      input, output

   processes
      Sender

   definitions
      Sender = input . output . Sender

   end Sender
```

The specification is given in the form of a *module*. The use of modules will be explained in more detail in the section on modularization. The *module* construct in this example serves three purposes:

- it groups a set of related entities, using a *begin-end* pair;
- it gives the type of the module: *process* (as opposed to a *data* module);
- it attaches a name to the module: *Sender*.

Within the module we see different sections. The *atoms* section defines a set of atomic actions by declaring their names. The *processes* section declares a set of process names. Finally, the processes are defined in the *definitions* section by relating a process name to a process expression using the '=' construct. In the example the behaviour of *Sender* is defined in terms of the two actions *input* and *output* and the process *Sender* itself. We should mention two technical points here:

- if there is more than one definition for a process in the *definitions* section, the different process expressions will be interpreted as *alternatives*. The concept of *alternatives* in PSF will be explained later.

- if a process name is declared but has not been defined, it is defined implicitly to be *deadlock*. The constant process expression *deadlock* will be described in the following section.

Although the language permits the usage of any valid identifier name for the different entities, we will adhere to some standard naming convention. This will help to distinguish between the different identifiers in a specification.

- a module name starts with an upper case character.
  example: *Sender*.

- an action name consists of lower case characters only.
  example: *input*.

- a process name starts with an upper case character.
  example: *Sender*.

2.4.1.6 Deadlock

Although *deadlock* will never literally appear in a PSF specification, we have to explain its behaviour. We can think of deadlock as a process expression describing a state, from which no progression can be made. In other words: deadlock is an *unsuccessful termination*. Because there are no actions that can evolve from a deadlock, we will not associate any action relation with it.

2.4.1.7 Sequential Composition

The process expression defining the behaviour of the process *Sender*, consists of atomic actions: *input* and *output*, the process *Sender* itself and the '·'-operator. This operator is called the *sequential composition*, and expresses the order in which events have to occur. The semantics for the sequential composition is given by the following action relations. The expressions above the line are conditions that must be met to conclude the expressions below the line.

$$\frac{x \xrightarrow{a} x'}{x{\cdot}y \xrightarrow{a} x'{\cdot}y} \qquad \frac{x \xrightarrow{a} \surd}{x{\cdot}y \xrightarrow{a} y}$$

Table 2.3   Action relations for sequential composition

The first rule says that whenever x can execute an a thereby evolving into x', $x{\cdot}y$ can perform this same a, and evolve into $x'{\cdot}y$. The second rule states that whenever x can terminate after having executed an a, the process $x{\cdot}y$ can evolve into y after an a.

In the example of the sender, the process expression *input · output · Sender* executes the action *input*, followed by *output*. The remaining part of the process expression, after these actions have been executed, is *Sender*.

2.4.1.8 Recursion

Process expressions can contain process names, as was shown in the previous section. The occurrence of such a process name is in fact an abbreviation for the process expression related to the process name as defined in the definitions section.

If the name of a process appears in its own definition, directly or indirectly through a chain of expansions of other process names, we call this phenomenon *recursion*. By using recursion it is possible to specify processes with an infinite behaviour by means of a finite set of finite definitions. The action relations describing recursion are given below. The X denotes the process name and x the process expression it represents. The symbol $\wedge$ represents logical conjunction.

$$\frac{X = x \ \wedge \ x \xrightarrow{a} x'}{X \xrightarrow{a} x'} \qquad \frac{X = x \ \wedge \ x \xrightarrow{a} \surd}{X \xrightarrow{a} \surd}$$

Table 2.4   Action relations for recursion

In the example the sender, which is an infinite process, is defined by means of recursion.

2.4.1.9 Alternative Composition

In the next specification we describe the channel from Figure 2.2. The channel we are going to specify allows for data to travel in one direction and has the possibility of losing the data it is transporting. The behaviour is described as follows: first the channel reads a datum at its input port, then it decides whether to pass it on to its output port correctly or incorrectly. Finally it returns to its initial state, waiting for the next datum to arrive at the input port.

```
process module Channel
begin

    atoms
        input, output, error

    processes
        Channel, Choice

    definitions
        Channel = input . Choice . Channel
        Choice = output + error

end Channel
```

The choice determining whether or not a datum is transported correctly is modelled by the process *Choice* through the use of the '+'-operator, the *alternative composition*. The process expression $x + y$ expresses a process that first chooses non-deterministically between x and y, and then continues with the execution of the chosen process. The semantics for the alternative composition are given by the following action rules:

$$\frac{x \xrightarrow{a} x'}{x+y \xrightarrow{a} x'} \qquad \frac{x \xrightarrow{a} \surd}{x+y \xrightarrow{a} \surd} \qquad \frac{y \xrightarrow{a} y'}{x+y \xrightarrow{a} y'} \qquad \frac{y \xrightarrow{a} \surd}{x+y \xrightarrow{a} \surd}$$

Table 2.5   Action relations for alternative composition

To complete the specification of the example we give the specification of the receiver. Its behaviour is described as follows. It has to anticipate the incorrect transmission of the datum through the channel. Therefore it can either perform an *input* or an *error* action in its initial state. If the *input* action occurs, a corresponding *output* action is performed and the process returns to its initial state. However, if the *error* action occurs the process returns to the initial state immediately, without performing any actions.

```
process module Receiver
begin

    atoms
        input, output, error

    processes
        Receiver
```

```
definitions
   Receiver = ((input . output) + error) . Receiver

end Receiver
```

The example shows that parentheses can be used in the process definition, to group expressions. The sequential composition binds stronger than the alternative composition, so in the example the inner pair of parentheses could have been left out.

2.4.1.10   Integrating Components

Now that we have given specifications for the different components of the system we need to integrate them. In this section we will combine them into one module. In the section on modularization we will discuss a different approach to integration.

The first problem that we encounter when we try to put the components in one module, is a naming problem. Each component in the original specification contained an *input* and an *output* action. If we simply took the union of the different sections, the name *input* would become ambiguous, because it would refer to three different atomic actions. This phenomenon is called a *name clash*. To overcome this problem we have to assign new names to the different atomic actions.

The specification of the complete system is given below. It contains some new language constructs, which will be explained in detail in the sections to come.

```
process module System
begin

   atoms
      sender-input, channel-input, receiver-input,
      sender-output, channel-output, receiver-output,
      channel-error, receiver-error,
      sender-to-channel, channel-to-receiver, error-transmission

   processes
      System, System', Sender, Channel, Receiver

   sets
      of atoms
         H = { sender-output, channel-input, channel-output,
               receiver-input, channel-error, receiver-error }
         I = { sender-to-channel, channel-to-receiver, error-transmission }

   communications
      sender-output | channel-input = sender-to-channel
      channel-output | receiver-input = channel-to-receiver
      channel-error | receiver-error = error-transmission

   definitions
      Sender = sender-input . sender-output . Sender
      Channel = channel-input .
                   (skip . channel-output + skip . channel-error) .
                Channel
      Receiver = ((receiver-input . receiver-output) + receiver-error) .
                   Receiver
```

```
System = encaps(H, Sender || Channel || Receiver)
System' = hide(I, System)
```

end System

2.4.1.11   Sets

The first new section that appears in the specification of the complete system is the *sets* section. In this case two *sets of atoms* are defined. Sets are merely a notational convenience and are used as parameters in certain *process operators*.

We can assign a name to a set, so that we do not have to repeat the contents of the set every time we want to refer to it. In the example, *H* and *I* are defined by an *enumeration* of the atomic actions that are part of the set. Moreover, there are three set operators: *union, intersection* and *difference*. The syntax for these operators is:

- enumeration : $\{s_1, s_2, ..., s_n\}$ s_i is a set element
- union : $S + T$ S and T are sets
- intersection : $S . T$
- difference : $S \setminus T$

The naming convention for sets is as follows:
- a set name starts with an upper case character.
  example: *H*.

It is also possible to define sets of things other than atoms. We will see examples of this at a later stage.

2.4.1.12   Communication

The other new section that appears in the example is the *communications* section. In this section the possibilities of communication between the different atomic actions are described.

In PSF communication is defined as the simultaneous occurrence of two atomic actions. As a result of the communication these two atomic actions are transformed into one new atomic action. The communication function, that shows which actions are allowed to communicate and what their result will be, is defined in the communications section. The communication definition $a \mid b = c$, states that the atomic actions a and b can communicate and that the resulting action will be c. We should make two technical remarks with respect to the definition of the communication function:

- for any pair of actions at most one resulting action can be defined.

- there are no communications possible, other than the ones that are explicitly defined.

2.4.1.13   Parallel Composition

The *definitions* section of the example introduces a new operator: the *parallel composition*. The expression $x \parallel y$ states that the processes x and y are executed in parallel. PSF is based on a so-called *interleaving* semantics for parallel composition. This means that either the left operand or the right operand performs an atomic action or that the initial actions from both operands communicate with each other. The action rules for parallel composition are:

$$\frac{x \xrightarrow{a} x'}{x \| y \xrightarrow{a} x' \| y} \qquad \frac{x \xrightarrow{a} \sqrt{}}{x \| y \xrightarrow{a} y} \qquad \frac{x \xrightarrow{a} x' \wedge y \xrightarrow{b} y' \wedge a \,|\, b = c}{x \| y \xrightarrow{c} x' \| y'} \qquad \frac{x \xrightarrow{a} \sqrt{} \wedge y \xrightarrow{b} y' \wedge a \,|\, b = c}{x \| y \xrightarrow{c} y'}$$

$$\frac{y \xrightarrow{a} y'}{x \| y \xrightarrow{a} x \| y'} \qquad \frac{y \xrightarrow{a} \sqrt{}}{x \| y \xrightarrow{a} x} \qquad \frac{x \xrightarrow{a} x' \wedge y \xrightarrow{b} \sqrt{} \wedge a \,|\, b = c}{x \| y \xrightarrow{c} x'} \qquad \frac{x \xrightarrow{a} \sqrt{} \wedge y \xrightarrow{b} \sqrt{} \wedge a \,|\, b = c}{x \| y \xrightarrow{c} \sqrt{}}$$

Table 2.6   Action relations for parallel composition

The parallel composition binds stronger than the alternative composition, but less strong than the sequential composition.

2.4.1.14   Encapsulation

The *encapsulation operator*, in the PSF specification written for example as: *encaps(H,x)*, is a specific instance of the general class of *renaming* operators. Renaming operators rename atomic actions into process expressions. The encapsulation operator takes as arguments a set of atoms H, and a process expression x. All atomic actions from H that appear in the process expression are renamed into *deadlock*. This is also true for actions that are the result of some communication that appears inside the process expression. The action relations are as follows:

$$\frac{x \xrightarrow{a} x' \wedge a \notin H}{\text{encaps}(H,x) \xrightarrow{a} \text{encaps}(H,x')} \qquad \frac{x \xrightarrow{a} \sqrt{} \wedge a \notin H}{\text{encaps}(H,x) \xrightarrow{a} \sqrt{}}$$

Table 2.7   Action relations for the encapsulation operator

There are no action relations for the case $a \in H$. The complete *encapsulation expression* has the same behaviour as *deadlock*, from which it is not possible to do any steps.

The main usage of the encapsulation operator is to guide the process of communication between two processes. In the previous section we have seen that the parallel composition of x and y is defined as the alternative composition of three other process expressions. Most of the time we want just one of the three alternatives to appear, namely the one in which an atomic action from x and an atomic action from y communicate. By adding the atomic actions that appear in x and y to the *encapsulation set*, we obstruct them from being performed as such, leaving only the possibility in which x and y have to communicate.

2.4.1.15   The Internal Step

The specification of the channel uses a new constant process expression: *skip*. This *skip* is an internal action of the system. We will encounter its main usage in the following section. The action rule for *skip* is:

$$\text{skip} \xrightarrow{\ skip\ } \sqrt{}$$

Table 2.8   Action relation for the internal step

In the running example *skip* is used to make sure that the choice between successful and unsuccessful transmission of the data is made non-deterministically. In other words, the choice can not be influenced by the outside world.

If we leave out the *skip* expressions, the receiver could influence the choice by offering only one of the possible partners in communication, thereby forcing a choice. Now the choice is made between two indistinguishable *skips*.

We should mention a technical point here. The expression *(skip · input) + (skip · error)* is not equivalent to *skip · (input + error)*. In other words: the left-distributivity does not hold, although the right-distributivity does. The difference stems from the fact that the *moment of choice* in both expressions is not the same.

In the first expression it is possible to choose between the expression *skip · input* or *skip · error*. However, the second expression offers the possibility of performing a *skip* first, and only then choosing between the expressions *input* or *error*. In the second case, the outside world would be able to influence the choice, in the way described above.

2.4.1.16   Abstraction

The *abstraction operator*, in the PSF specification written as *hide(I,x)*, is closely related to the encapsulation operator. The abstraction operator renames atomic actions, contained in its set argument *I*, into *skip*. The action rules are as follows:

$$\frac{x \xrightarrow{a} x' \wedge a \in I}{\text{hide}(I,x) \xrightarrow{\ skip\ } \text{hide}(I,x')} \qquad \frac{x \xrightarrow{a} \sqrt{} \wedge a \in I}{\text{hide}(I,x) \xrightarrow{\ skip\ } \sqrt{}}$$

$$\frac{x \xrightarrow{a} x' \wedge a \notin I}{\text{hide}(I,x) \xrightarrow{a} \text{hide}(I,x')} \qquad \frac{x \xrightarrow{a} \sqrt{} \wedge a \notin I}{\text{hide}(I,x) \xrightarrow{a} \sqrt{}}$$

Table 2.9   Action relations for the abstraction operator

The main usage of the abstraction operator is connected with the process of communication. In a large number of specifications we are not interested in the result of all the communication actions. A lot of communication actions are just used internally to synchronize two or more processes. When investigating the behaviour of a process, we are mostly interested in the *external* behaviour. This means that we want to abstract from all *internal* activity. We can achieve this effect by renaming all atomic actions, representing details we are not interested in, into *skip*.

As suggested before, the *abstraction operator* and *encapsulation operator* are mostly used in cooperation. A typical example of such a cooperation is:

hide(I, encaps(H, ...))

In the running example we have also used this construct to specify the process *System'*. We abstract from all internal communications between the sender, the channel and the receiver (*sender-to-channel, channel-to-receiver, error-transmission*). These actions form the set *I*. The set *H* consists of all atomic actions that take part in the communications that result in the actions from set *I*. By encapsulating the actions from *H* we force communication between them. The result is that in *System'* the only observable behaviour consists of the actions *sender-input* and *receiver-output* and of the constant process expression *skip*.

2.4.1.17   Summary of the Process Part of PSF

In this section we will give a graphical representation of the relation between the concepts we have introduced so far. The ellipses represent the different domains we have explained. The arrows suggest the different functions that take elements from a domain (the dots), and produce an entity in another domain (the arrow head).

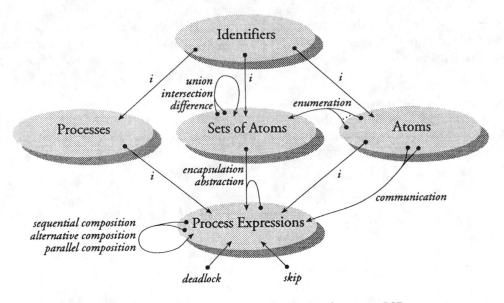

Figure 2.3   Graphical representation of relations between PSF concepts

The function *i* represents the *injection* function. The injection function is an *implicit, invisible,* function application. To clarify this notion we will give an example.

The string *a* is an identifier. Moreover it can be the name of a process, a set or an atomic action. Whenever it is a name for a process or atomic action, it is also a process expression representing the corresponding process or atomic action. Its type is derived from the context in which it is used.

2.4.2   MODULARIZATION

In the previous section we have integrated different components by combining them into one module. This method is rather cumbersome and becomes more and more complicated as the size of the specification grows. PSF supports the use of several modularization techniques, which will be discussed in the sequel.

2.4.2.1 Modules
In the previous specifications we have already used the *module* concept. Each specification consisted of exactly one module. A PSF specification in general consists of a series of modules. Modules can depend on objects defined in other modules, so there exists a certain relation between them.

2.4.2.2 Exports
The first step towards modular design is to divide all the entities in a module into two categories. One category for the objects that are visible to the world outside a module, the *exported objects*, and one for those objects that are used only locally, the *hidden objects*.

In PSF the exported objects are surrounded by a *begin-end* pair that follows the *exports* keyword. All other objects that are defined are hidden. In the two examples below all objects are exported. The two examples redefine the *Sender* and *Receiver* processes we have defined earlier.

```
process module  Sender
begin

  exports
    begin
      atoms
        input, output
      processes
        Sender
    end

  definitions
    Sender = input . output . Sender

end Sender

process module  Receiver
begin

  exports
    begin
      atoms
        input, output, error
      processes
        Receiver
    end

  definitions
    Receiver = ((input . output) + error) . Receiver

end Receiver
```

2.4.2.3 Hidden Objects

To show the use of *hidden* objects we give the specification of a module in which the exported process is defined in terms of an *auxiliary* process. Because of its very specific nature, this auxiliary process is intended to be local to the module. This feature of shielding functions and data from the outside world is also known as .i.*information hiding* ;or .i.*data encapsulation*;. The term *hidden* in the context of modularization should not be confused with *hide*, the representation of the abstraction operator in PSF. The following example redefines the *Channel* process.

```
process module  Channel
begin

  exports
    begin
      atoms
        input, output, error
      processes
        Channel
    end

  processes
    Choice

  definitions
    Channel = input . Choice . Channel
    Choice = (skip . output) + (skip . error)

end Channel
```

The process *Choice* is the local process, used in the definition of *Channel*. It is not meant to be known to the outside world and therefore declared to be hidden. We recall that all entities that are not explicitly named in the *exports* section are hidden.

2.4.2.4 Importing Modules & Renaming Objects

Now we will show how the three modules we have defined in the previous sections can be combined by means of *imports*, into one module called *System*.

```
process module  System
begin

  exports
    begin
      atoms
        sender-to-channel, channel-to-receiver, error-transmission
      processes
        System, System'
    end

  imports
    Sender {
      renamed by [
        input -> sender-input,
```

```
            output -> sender-output
        ]
      },
      Channel {
        renamed by [
          input -> channel-input,
          output -> channel-output,
          error -> channel-error
        ]
      },
      Receiver {
        renamed by [
          input -> receiver-input,
          output -> receiver-output,
          error -> receiver-error
        ]
      }

  sets
    of atoms
      H = { sender-output, channel-input, channel-output,
            receiver-input, channel-error, receiver-error }
      I = { sender-to-channel, channel-to-receiver, error-transmission }

  communications
    sender-output | channel-input = sender-to-channel
    channel-output | receiver-input = channel-to-receiver
    channel-error | receiver-error = error-transmission

  definitions
    System = encaps(H, Sender || Channel || Receiver)
    System' = hide(I, System)

end System
```

In the example above, the exported objects from the module *Sender* are made available to *System* by importing *Sender*. The imported modules are given as a list of modules preceded by the *imports* keyword.

In the example we see that every module name is followed by a list of *renamings*. The renamings first specify the name of the object in the module of origin, and then the name in the current module. If an object is not renamed in the renaming list, it keeps its old name.

Although renaming is optional, in the example we have to rename the atomic actions coming from the imported modules, because otherwise we would run into a name clash, as was explained above.

All objects that are imported into a module, are implicitly imported into its export section. This means for example, that any module that imports module *System* will automatically be able to use the action *sender-input* from module *Sender*.

2.4.3   DATA MODULES & PARAMETERIZATION

Until now we have given examples in which we have been abstracting from what
was sent from the sender to the receiver. We have been describing the behaviour of
the system for an abstract message. If we want to model our example on a higher
level of detail, we have to be able to add data parameters to the atomic actions and
processes. In the following sections we will show how data is modelled in PSF, and
how it is incorporated into the processes. Moreover, we will show how a module can
be parameterized with elements from the data domain.

2.4.3.1 Sorts & Functions

Data in PSF is specified using a so-called equational specification. The entities that
are used in such specifications are *sorts* and *functions*. In the example below we give
the specification of the *booleans*.

```
data module Booleans
begin

  exports
    begin
      sorts
        BOOLEAN
      functions
        true : -> BOOLEAN
        false : -> BOOLEAN
    end

  end Booleans
```

As opposed to the process modules, a data module is preceded by the keyword: *data*.
In the example we see that there are two new sections. The *sorts* section introduces
sorts or data domains, and the functions section declares functions that operate on
elements from these data domains.

The example defines one sort: *BOOLEAN*, and two functions *true* and *false*. The
naming convention follows from the example:

- a sort name consists of upper case characters only.
  example: *BOOLEAN*.

- a function name consists of lower case characters only.
  example: *true*.

A function declaration has the following general appearance:

function-name : *input type* -> *output type*

The clause *input type* is a list of sorts separated by '#'-symbols and *output type* is a
sort. The input type specifies the types of the arguments of the function, and the
output specifies the type of the result. The two functions in the example have no
input type and are so-called *constant functions*.

2.4.3.2 Equations

The behaviour of functions is given by means of equations. In an equation we actually specify that two terms are equivalent. In the implementation however, an equation is interpreted as a rule from a *term rewriting system*, in which the left-hand side is rewritten to the right-hand side. In the example below we will give a specification of a module containing some messages.

```
data module Messages
begin

  exports
    begin
      sorts
        MESSAGE
      functions
        message-error : -> MESSAGE
        message-1 : -> MESSAGE
        message-2 : -> MESSAGE
        message-3 : -> MESSAGE
        valid : MESSAGE -> BOOLEAN
    end

  imports
    Booleans

  equations
  [01] valid(message-error) = false
  [02] valid(message-1) = true
  [03] valid(message-2) = true
  [04] valid(message-3) = true

end Messages
```

We have introduced the sort *MESSAGE*, that contains four messages. One of these items represents a message that has been garbled: *message-error*. To be able to distinguish between valid and invalid messages we have defined a function *valid*, which accepts a message as input and which yields the boolean value *true* for an ordinary message, and *false* for a garbled message. The usage of the function *valid* will be illustrated in one of the following sections.

2.4.3.3 Initial Algebra Semantics

In the previous sections we have been assigning semantics to all language constructs we have introduced using *action relations*. The data type specifications in PSF are interpreted using *initial algebra* semantics. We will only sketch the principles of the initial algebra of a specification here, for a more detailed explanation we refer to the literature.

Using the functions introduced in a data type specification it is possible to construct *terms*. Two examples of simple *terms* of type *BOOLEAN*, from module *Booleans*, are *true* and *false*.

Module *Messages* introduces four constant functions of type *MESSAGE* and a function *valid* with *MESSAGE* as input type and *BOOLEAN* as output type. Using *valid* it is possible to create four new terms of type *BOOLEAN*: *valid(message-error)*, *valid(message-1)*, *valid(message-2)* and *valid(message-3)*. This implies that there are six different terms of type *BOOLEAN* in module *Messages*, the four created using *valid*, plus the two already introduced in *Booleans*.

Not all these terms refer to different entities. One of the equations in *Messages* states that *valid(message-1)* is equal to *true*. We say that *valid(message-1)* and *true* refer to the same element in the *initial algebra* of *BOOLEAN*.

We conclude with an informal method to determine the initial algebra of a sort. The first step is to generate all possible terms of a given sort. The result is a possibly infinite set of data terms. In the second step all terms that are equal, according to the given equations, are grouped together. The result is that the set of terms is divided in so-called *equivalence classes*. Each equivalence class is exactly one element of the initial algebra. One of the terms in the equivalence class is chosen to be the *representant* of the given equivalence class. The following figure shows the abovementioned procedure for the sort *BOOLEAN*.

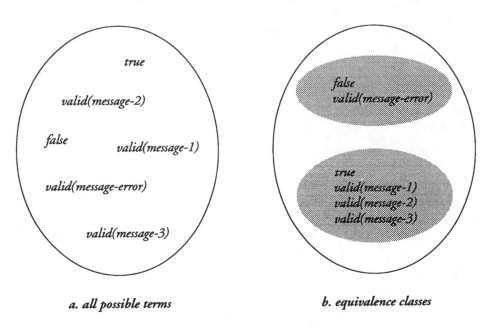

a. all possible terms   b. equivalence classes

Figure 2.4   Determining the initial algebra

2.4.3.4 Parameterization of Actions and Processes
The data introduced in the previous section, is integrated into the process domain, by allowing processes and actions to be parameterized with tuples of data elements. Or to put it in a different way, processes and actions can have data items as arguments.

To show the use of these data parameters, and not have to introduce too many new concepts at once, we briefly leave our running example and turn to a specification of a memory cell that can contain one *boolean* value. First we will give a graphical representation of this memory cell.

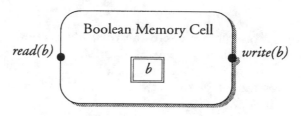

Figure 2.5   Boolean Memory Cell

The behaviour of the memory cell is as follows. In the initial state it is only capable of reading a boolean value performing the action *read*. After having read a value it can either input a new value or it can show the value it contains by performing the action *write*. The actions will be parameterized by a boolean value.

Keep in mind that this is a specification of a memory cell from the point of perspective of the cell itself. So *read* does *not* mean reading the memory cell but assigning a value to the memory cell.

```
process module Boolean-Cell
begin

   imports
     Booleans

   atoms
     read, write : BOOLEAN

   processes
     Cell
     Cell : BOOLEAN

   variables
     b : -> BOOLEAN

   definitions
     Cell    = sum(v in BOOLEAN, read(v) . Cell(v))
     Cell(b) = write(b) . Cell(b) + Cell

  end Boolean-Cell
```

Arguments of an action or process are written between parentheses, as shown in the example. The actions *read* and *write* are declared to have a boolean argument. There are two instances of the process *Cell*, one with a boolean parameter, and one with no parameters. This is an example of a phenomenon called *overloading*.

2.4.3.5 Overloading of Identifiers

The name *Cell* is overloaded, because it can refer to two different processes. PSF allows overloading of the names of entities as long as the entities can be distinguished by the types of their parameters. Entities that cannot contain parameters, like sorts for instance, cannot be overloaded.

2.4.3.6 Variables

The example introduces one new section: the *variables* section. In this section we define the type of the variables that are used in the process definitions. In this example the process *Cell(b)* uses its parameter *b*, a boolean variable, to remember its current value. Variables cannot be exported and are therefore always local to the module in which they are defined.

2.4.3.7 Generalized Alternative and Parallel Composition

The final point of interest in the example of the memory cell, is the usage of the generalized alternative composition: *sum(v in BOOLEAN, ...)*. The general appearance of the generalized alternative composition is: *sum(x in S, P)*. The *S* can be a *sort* or a *data* set. The *x* is called a *placeholder* and represents an element from the data domain of *S*. The expression *sum(x in S, P)* is an abbreviation of an alternative composition containing, for every possible *valuation* of *x*, a copy of *P* in which *x* is replaced by the valuation of *x*:

$$P[x/s_1] + \ldots + P[x/s_n]$$

As an example of this substitution we give the evaluation of the definition of *Cell* from the example:

$$read(true) \,.\, Cell(true) + read(false) \,.\, Cell(false)$$

In the same way we define the generalized parallel composition, which is denoted by *merge(x in S, P)*.

The specification of the memory cell represents a system that can be in any of three states: *Cell*, *Cell(false)* and *Cell(true)*. Below we will give a picture of the states and the possible transitions between them.

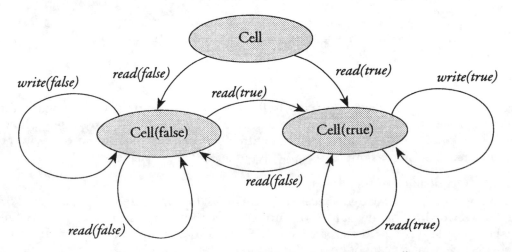

Figure 2.6   States and transitions of the memory cell

2.4.3.8 Parameterization of a Module

In the previous sections we have shown how a data element can be a parameter of a process or an atomic action. In this section we will focus on parameterization on a different level, namely on the level of modules.

In the approach we took for the specification of the memory cell, we specified a cell that explicitly deals with booleans. If we would like a specification of a cell that remembers natural numbers, we would have to give a complete new specification. This is of course inconvenient, and therefore PSF incorporates a mechanism that enables us to give a specification of a process that operates on a certain data type, although that type itself is not yet fully specified.

The *Sender* process is a good candidate for parameterization, because in essence it is capable of sending all kinds of objects. Therefore, we can make the data type a parameter of the module.

```
process module  Sender
begin

   parameters
     Sender-Parameter
     begin
        sorts
          DATA
     end Sender-Parameter

   exports
     begin
       atoms
         input : DATA
         output : DATA
       processes
         Sender
     end

   definitions
     Sender = sum(d in DATA, input(d) . output(d)) . Sender

end Sender
```

In the example above we can see that parameters are introduced in the *parameters* section. The entries in the *parameters* section are *named parameter blocks*. The name of the parameter block in the example is Sender-Parameter. Each block can contain *sorts, functions, sets, atoms* and *processes*. The entities that are introduced in the parameters section, are treated in the rest of the module as if they were normal entities.

Not all processes can be parameterized in such a simple way as described above. The *Sender* does not *depend* on the data it is transporting. On the contrary, a process that would sort items *does* depend on the data it is sorting, because it has to know the order of two data items. In such cases, the module that defines the sorting process still can be parameterized, but the ordering function must also be part of the parameter.

The following specification of the *Channel* also shows such a dependency. The channel can transport a datum correctly or the datum can get garbled. In the latter case the channel has to output a special *error element* of type *DATA*. This error element is therefore part of the parameter of *Channel*.

```
process module  Channel
begin

  parameters
    Channel-Parameter
    begin
      sorts
        DATA
      functions
        error : -> DATA
    end Channel-Parameter

  exports
    begin
      atoms
        input : DATA
        output : DATA
      processes
        Channel
    end

  processes
    Choice : DATA

  variables
    d : -> DATA

  definitions
    Channel = sum(d in DATA, input(d) . Choice(d)) . Channel
    Choice(d) = (skip . output(d)) + (skip . output(error))

  end Channel
```

2.4.3.9 Conditional Expressions

The specification of the *receiver* with data parameters, requires a new language construct, the *conditional expression*. This construct is used to make choices, based on the data terms, which influence the behaviour of the process. In the example below the *conditional expression* is used to check the validity of the incoming data, and to respond to it in different ways.

```
process module  Receiver
begin

  parameters
    Receiver-Parameter
```

```
      begin
        sorts
          DATA
        functions
          valid-data : DATA -> BOOLEAN
      end Receiver-Parameter

  exports
    begin
      atoms
        input : DATA
        output : DATA
      processes
        Receiver
    end

  imports
    Booleans

  processes
    Validate : DATA

  variables
    d : -> DATA

  definitions
    Receiver = sum(d in DATA, input(d) . Validate(d))
    Validate(d) = [valid-data(d) = true] -> output(d) . Receiver +
                  [valid-data(d) = false] -> Receiver

end Receiver
```

Each process expression can be prefixed by a conditional expression $[s = t] \rightarrow P$. The expression $[s = t]$ is also called a *guard*. If s and t are equal, according to the initial algebra, we say that the guard is *true*, if they are not equal the guard is *false*. If the guard of $[s = t] \rightarrow P$ is true, the conditional expression evaluates to process P. If the guard is false, the conditional expression evaluates to *deadlock*. The semantics is given below.

$$\frac{x \xrightarrow{a} x' \wedge s = t}{([s = t] \rightarrow x) \xrightarrow{a} x'} \qquad \frac{x \xrightarrow{a} \surd \wedge s = t}{([s = t] \rightarrow x) \xrightarrow{a} \surd}$$

Table 2.10 Action relations for the conditional expression

2.4.3.10 Binding of Parameters

After having carried out such a conscientious preparation, we are finally able to create a completed specification of the interaction between the sender, the channel and the receiver. We achieve our final specification of the example by binding all the parameters, the *formal* entities, in the specification to *actual* entities. In the following example the sort *DATA*, which was the parameter representing the type

of the objects that are handled by the protocol, is bound to the sort *MESSAGE* of the
module *Messages*.

```
process module  System
begin

  exports
    begin
      atoms
        sender-to-channel : MESSAGE
        channel-to-receiver : MESSAGE
      processes
        System, System'
    end

  imports
    Sender {
      Sender-Parameter bound by [
        DATA -> MESSAGE
      ] to Messages
      renamed by [
        input -> sender-input,
        output -> sender-output
      ]
    },
    Channel {
      Channel-Parameter bound by [
        DATA -> MESSAGE,
        error -> message-error
      ] to Messages
      renamed by [
        input -> channel-input,
        output -> channel-output
      ]
    },
    Receiver {
      Receiver-Parameter bound by [
        DATA -> MESSAGE,
        valid-data -> valid
      ] to Messages
      renamed by [
        input -> receiver-input,
        output -> receiver-output
      ]
    }

  sets
    of atoms
      H = { sender-output(m), channel-input(m), channel-output(m),
            receiver-input(m) | m in MESSAGE }
      I = { sender-to-channel(m), channel-to-receiver(m) |
            m in MESSAGE }

  communications
    sender-output(m) | channel-input(m) = sender-to-channel(m)
      for m in MESSAGE
```

```
channel-output(m) | receiver-input(m) = channel-to-receiver(m)
   for m in MESSAGE

definitions
  System = encaps(H, Sender || Channel || Receiver)
  System' = hide(I, System)

end System
```

In the example we can see that the binding of a parameter is achieved by importing a module *A*, that contains a parameter and binding it to a module *B*. The formal objects from module *A* are bound to the actual objects of module *B* by means of a syntactical construct that resembles the renaming construct. Any parameter blocks of an imported module that are not bound, are *inherited* by the importing module. This means that the unbound parameter blocks are added to the set of parameter blocks of the latter module.

Furthermore, this example shows that the definition of a set and the definition of a communication can be parameterized with a variable. Below we give an example of the syntax:

- set definition: $S = \{ a(x) \mid x \; in \; T \}$
- communication definition: $a(x) \mid b(x) = c(x) \; for \; x \; in \; T$

We should make one final remark about this specification. In the example we bind *message-error*, an element from *MESSAGE*, to the *error* parameter of *Channel*. This means that if the message gets garbled within the channel, *Channel* will use *message-error* to indicate this fact. However, this is not the only situation in which *Receiver* can receive a *message-error*. Because *message-error* is an element of *MESSAGE*, it can be sent directly by the sender as well.

2.5   THE PSF STANDARD LIBRARY

In the previous sections we have been referring to the PSF Standard Library. This library contains some frequently used data types. Using this library has two great advantages. The first being the fact that a specification can be built upon already existing reusable modules, in other words a specification does not have to be given from scratch. The other advantage is a certain uniformity in the specifications given, because they are based on the same set of basic modules.

In this section we will give a short description of the data types in this library that are used throughout this book. Each entry will only show the exported sorts and functions, which is also called the *export signature*. After the signature we will list the initial algebra of the data type being defined, one example term from this module and its normal form. The complete listings of the relevant part of the PSF Standard Library can be found in Appendix A.

2.5.1   BOOLEANS

One of the simpler data types is the boolean. The standard library defines the sort *BOOLEAN*.

```
sorts
  BOOLEAN
functions
  true  :                           -> BOOLEAN
  false :                           -> BOOLEAN
  eq    : BOOLEAN # BOOLEAN -> BOOLEAN      -- equality
  not   : BOOLEAN           -> BOOLEAN
  and   : BOOLEAN # BOOLEAN -> BOOLEAN
  or    : BOOLEAN # BOOLEAN -> BOOLEAN
  xor   : BOOLEAN # BOOLEAN -> BOOLEAN      -- exclusive or
```

Initial Algebra: false, true.

Example Term: and(true,or(false,true)) $\rightarrow$ true

2.5.2   NATURALS

The simplest way to represent the natural numbers is by so-called *successor naturals*. There is one constant function *zero*, and all other natural numbers are constructed by applying the successor function *s* one or more times to *zero*.

There are three *infix* operators in this signature: _+_ , _-_ and _*_. They represent addition, subtraction and multiplication. The two underscores '_' indicate the place of their arguments.

```
sorts
  NATURAL
functions
  zero :                    -> NATURAL
  s    : NATURAL            -> NATURAL
  eq   : NATURAL # NATURAL -> BOOLEAN
  gte  : NATURAL # NATURAL -> BOOLEAN
  gt   : NATURAL # NATURAL -> BOOLEAN
  lte  : NATURAL # NATURAL -> BOOLEAN
  lt   : NATURAL # NATURAL -> BOOLEAN
  inc  : NATURAL            -> NATURAL
  dec  : NATURAL            -> NATURAL
  _+_  : NATURAL # NATURAL -> NATURAL
  _-_  : NATURAL # NATURAL -> NATURAL
  _*_  : NATURAL # NATURAL -> NATURAL
  mod  : NATURAL # NATURAL -> NATURAL
  div  : NATURAL # NATURAL -> NATURAL
```

Initial Algebra: zero, s(zero), s(s(zero)), s(s(s(zero))), ...

Example Term: s(s(zero)) + s(s(s(zero))) $\rightarrow$ s(s(s(s(s(zero)))))

2.5.3   BITS

Computers use bits as the basic entity to represent information. The standard library defines two bits: *bit0, bit1*. Because of the fact that constants cannot be overloaded and that the identifier names *0* and *1* are used in the library to represent the digits, we have to introduce a different name for the bits.

```
sorts
  BIT
functions
  bit0    :                 -> BIT
  bit1    :                 -> BIT
  invert  : BIT             -> BIT
  unary   : BIT             -> NATURAL
  eq      : BIT # BIT -> BOOLEAN
```

Initial Algebra: bit0, bit1.

Example Terms: invert(bit0)   →   bit1

unary(bit1)   →   s(zero)

2.5.4   QUEUES

Queues are a well-known data structure. They are used to store data in a certain order. The standard library defines functions to put an item into a queue, to retrieve the front element from the queue, to delete the front element from the queue and to determine the number of items in a queue.

All functions are defined relative to the parameters of the module: *Q-ELEMENT* and *default-element*.

```
parameters
  sorts
    Q-ELEMENT
  functions
    default-q-element : -> Q-ELEMENT

sorts
  QUEUE
functions
  empty-queue :                          -> QUEUE
  enqueue     : Q-ELEMENT # QUEUE -> QUEUE
  serve       : QUEUE                    -> Q-ELEMENT
  dequeue     : QUEUE                    -> QUEUE
  length      : QUEUE                    -> NATURAL
  _*_         : Q-ELEMENT # QUEUE -> QUEUE
```

Initial Algebra: empty-queue, d1 * empty-queue, d2 * d1 * empty-queue, ...

Example Terms: dequeue(d2 * d1 * empty-queue)   →   d2 * empty-queue

serve(d2 * d1 * empty-queue)   →   d1

2.5.5   TABLES

Tables are a way to represent *dynamic arrays* in PSF. In fact the table data structure is more flexible, because the index can be of any type. When an item is stored into a table it is stored together with its *key*. The item itself can later be retrieved by supplying the *key* to the appropriate function. The standard library defines functions to put an item and its key into a table, to retrieve an item from a table, to delete an item from a table, to test whether or not a certain key is an element of a table, and to determine the number of items in a table.

All functions are defined relative to the parameters of the module, the sorts *KEY* and *ITEM* and the functions *eq* and *default-item*.

```
parameters
  sorts
    KEY
    ITEM
  functions
    eq            : KEY # KEY -> BOOLEAN
    default-item :             -> ITEM


sorts
  TABLE
functions
  empty-table :                     -> TABLE
  insert      : TABLE # ITEM # KEY  -> TABLE
  retrieve    : TABLE # KEY         -> ITEM
  delete      : TABLE # KEY         -> TABLE
  in-table    : TABLE # KEY         -> BOOLEAN
  length      : TABLE               -> NATURAL
  entry       : KEY # ITEM          -> ENTRY
  _ * _       : ENTRY # TABLE       -> TABLE
```

Initial Algebra: empty-table, entry(*k1*,*i1*) * empty-table,
                     entry(*k2*,*i2*) * entry(*k1*,*i1*) * empty-table, …

Example Term: delete(entry(*k2*,*i2*) * entry(*k1*,*i1*) * empty-table, *k1*)
                     → entry(*k2*,*i2*) * empty-table

2.5.6   DATA

The protocol specifications in this book make no assumptions about the kind of data they are transporting. By importing the module *Data* from the PSF Standard Library any module inherits a sort parameter *DATA* and a constant function *default-data*. This way modules can define parameters in a uniform way.

```
parameters
  sorts
    DATA
  functions
    default-data : -> DATA
```

2.6   THE PSF-TOOLKIT

The PSF-Toolkit consists of a number of programs that form a programming environment for the language PSF. The graphical representation of the system is given in Figure 2.7.

Situated at the centre of the PSF-Toolkit is the Tool Interface Language (TIL) through which all tools can communicate. This means that the tools in the PSF-

Toolkit do not directly operate on PSF but on a language on a lower level, which is represented by TIL. This language can be seen as an *assembler language* for an *abstract process algebra machine*. Because TIL is optimized for use by computers, its readability for humans is of secondary importance.

From the picture we see that the PSF specification at the top is translated into TIL by the PSF compiler. At the bottom of the picture we see the different tools. At present a simulator, a term rewriter, a proof assistant, an equivalence tester, an initial algebra generator and a transition system generator are implemented.

The approach of implementing an environment, by using clearly defined intermediate languages, serves several purposes. The main reason is that it results in a layered design, in which human users can inspect specifications on a high level through PSF and in which the tools have access to the specifications through a low level representation tailored to their needs. This means in particular that the process of parsing and type checking of PSF is of no concern to the tools which will use a very simple parser to read the intermediate language.

The second reason for using TIL and its derivatives is that software can be developed in parallel and independently, because there is an exact definition of the intermediate language. In the case of the PSF-Toolkit the construction of the simulator did not have to wait for the implementation of the parser and normalizer to be completed.

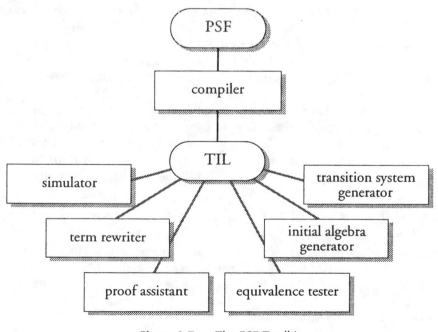

Figure 2.7   The PSF-Toolkit

The final reason for using TIL is that the PSF-Toolkit can be easily adapted for new versions of PSF, or formalisms with comparable functionality. Writing a parser that translates a formalism into M-TIL is sufficient to make all tools in the PSF-Toolkit available. This way, reusability of large parts of software, present in the tools, is guaranteed. At the moment two such alternative front-ends exist.

The following sections describe the implementation of the PSF-Toolkit, its languages and its tools in more detail. Readers that are mainly interested in the specifications of the communication protocols can safely skip this part, because the protocol specifications can be understood without the following information.

2.6.1   THE PSF COMPILER

The PSF compiler, called *psf*, translates PSF specifications into TIL specifications. The input for *psf* is a file containing one or more PSF modules. The compiler starts by determining the import structure of the specification. It creates a sorted list of modules, called the *import list*, such that, if module *A* imports module *B*, *B* occurs on the import list before *A*. The reason for this is that because module *A* depends on *B*, *B* must be compiled before *A*. If *psf* is not able to find such an ordering, execution is stopped and an error message is generated.

During the construction of the import list, *psf* starts its search for PSF modules in the input file. If the requested modules can not be found there, it looks for suitable files in the current directory. If this fails too, *psf* searches in the PSF Standard Library and a number of libraries that the user can specify.

Although the compiler acts like one program to the user of the system, internally it consists of several programs, a *parser*, a *normalizer/type checker* and a *library manager*. In the second phase *psf* starts to invoke the parser and normalizer/type checker with different arguments for each PSF module, in the order dictated by the import list. The intermediate files produced by these programs are not discarded but stored by the library manager, so they can be used again during subsequent calls to *psf*. The final result of a compilation is a TIL file, which is stored in the directory from which *psf* was called.

The library manager keeps track of the files that have been changed since the latest compilation by inspecting the time stamps that the operating system attaches to the physical files. This way the library manager can guarantee that on successive calls to *psf*, only those files that have been edited, or files that depend on edited files, are recompiled. This means that *psf* implements *separate compilation* of PSF files.

2.6.2   TERM REWRITING

The evaluation of the equality of data types, according to the initial algebra semantics, is implemented in PSF using a technique called *term rewriting*. In this section we will give a brief description of the basics of term rewriting. For more detailed information we refer to the literature.

Term rewriting is a sequence of transformations of a data term. The possible transformations are dictated by the equations given for a data type. The first step in rewriting a term *t*, consists of finding a sub-term *s* of *t* which *matches* one of the left-hand sides of the equations. Such a sub-term *s* is called a *redex* of *t*. As a result of matching, possible variables in the equation are bound to sub-terms of *s*. In the second step of rewriting, the occurrence of *s* in *t* is replaced by the right-hand side of the matching equation to form a new term t'. This process is repeated for the new term t' until no more matching left-hand sides of equations can be found. The resulting term is said to be in *normal form*.

We will illustrate this technique by means of an example in which we use the following specification of the *booleans*.

```
data module Booleans
begin

  sorts
    BOOLEAN

  functions
    true : -> BOOLEAN
    false : -> BOOLEAN
    not : BOOLEAN -> BOOLEAN
    and : BOOLEAN # BOOLEAN -> BOOLEAN
    or : BOOLEAN # BOOLEAN -> BOOLEAN

  variables
    x : -> BOOLEAN

  equations
  [01] not(true) = false
  [02] not(false) = true
  [03] and(true, x) - x
  [04] and(false, x) = false
  [05] or(true, x) = true
  [06] or(false, x) = x

end Booleans
```

In this example we will rewrite the term *and(true,false)*. The only redex is the complete term, which matches the left-hand side of equation *[03]*. As a result of the matching process, variable x will be bound to *false*. In the next step the redex is replaced by the right-hand side of equation *[03]*. The result is that *and(true,false)* is transformed into *false*. There are no redexes in *false*, so it is a normal form. The following section contains a more complicated example of term rewriting.

2.6.3 THE TERM REWRITER

The term rewriter in the PSF-Toolkit is a standard term rewriting program supporting *conditional equations*. The kernel of the term rewriter is used by the other programs in the PSF-Toolkit. We do not describe this usage here but we will focus on the use of the term rewriter as a stand-alone program.

The PSF language and the Toolkit can be used just as an algebraic specification environment. By specifying only data modules one can treat the PSF-Toolkit as an implementation of an algebraic specification language. The PSF-Toolkit has been used as such for several years now in courses on Algebraic Specification Methods at the University of Amsterdam.

The term rewriter takes as input a TIL file that specifies the sorts, functions and equations used in the specification. The terms to be rewritten are given in a second input file or are supplied interactively. The program offers a *trace* option to let the user inspect which rewrite rules are applied and what the intermediate results are. Below we will give an example of such a *trace* produced by the term rewriter. In this case a term is reduced using the specification of the booleans from the previous section.

```
and(true,or(not(false),not(true)))        =
    not(true)
    -> false
    not(false)
    -> true
    or(true,false)
    -> true
    and(true,true)
    -> true
true
```

The current implementation of the term rewriter uses a *rightmost-innermost* rewriting strategy, which can be deduced from the trace of rewrites. The term *innermost* in this context means that the term rewriter tries to find the innermost redexes first. If there is more than one such innermost redex, it reduces the redexes from right to left. This implies that rewriting is started at the *rightmost* redex. We give a picture of the process of rewriting of the example to illustrate this strategy.

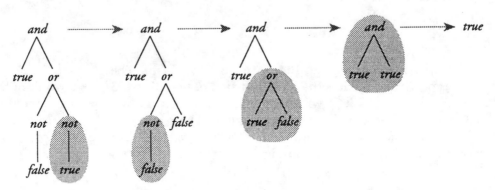

Figure 2.8   The rightmost-innermost reduction strategy

2.6.4   THE SIMULATOR

The main purpose of the simulator is to show a possible trace of the behaviour of a process. There are several windows that are used to communicate with the user. There is a window that contains the specification in PSF format, another window is used to display the trace of atomic actions, and one window is used for special system messages. Furthermore, there are two windows containing a number of buttons with which the user can command the simulator.

Initially the simulator shows all the processes that are defined in its TIL input file and asks the user to select the process from which the simulation has to start. Then a menu containing a series of possible atomic actions to be performed is shown and the user has the possibility to select one of these actions. The simulator also offers the possibility to make a random choice from this menu. Moreover it is possible to let the simulator make a choice at each point in time. So the simulator can generate random traces from the state space. In this case execution halts when the simulated process has finished, deadlocked or when the random choice mode is deselected.

The simulator offers two possible trace options. The one most commonly used is the option in which only the actions, visible to the outside world as defined in the specification, are shown. The visibility is governed by the use of the *encapsulation* and *abstraction* operators in the specification. The other trace option allows for selecting any atomic action or process identifier in the specification to be traced, irrespective of its visibility. The trace that has been accumulated during a simulation of a process can be exported to a file.

To facilitate the process of spotting errors in a specification, the simulator offers the possibility to set a breakpoint on the execution of an atomic action. In this mode of operation the simulator can be compared with a source level debugger for a conventional programming language.

2.6.5   THE PROOF ASSISTANT

The proof assistant is in fact a *desk calculator* for process expressions. Process expressions can be manipulated at a syntactical level and proven to be equal to other process expressions. The proof assistant uses a set of axioms that define the permitted transformations.

Trying to prove facts about process expressions by using only the axioms provided can be a tiresome job. As a typical example: we found in one of our first experiments with the initial implementation of the proof assistant, that a simple proof, which takes seven steps when done with pencil and paper, takes more than sixty steps when applying only one axiom at a time. It goes without saying that a successful proof assistant should provide means to shorten such proofs. The proof assistant in the PSF-Toolkit tries to cope with this problem by imitating some of the reasoning used by human provers. The resulting strategies are called *tactics*.

The proof assistant uses a TIL specification as input and interacts with the user through a number of windows. Initially the proof assistant lets the user choose one process from a menu containing all left-hand sides of the process definitions from the TIL input file. This process identifier is shown in a window that will hold the proof and is expanded to its right-hand side.

Now the user can select a subterm of this expanded expression, and the proof assistant will show the possible rewrites that can be applied to this subterm or will offer the possibility of *expansion* when a process identifier was chosen. Moreover, it is possible to apply one of the above-mentioned *tactics* to the selected term. The selected subterm is transformed according to the actions of the user, and the resulting process expression is written on a new line, after which the process of selecting and transforming can be repeated.

2.6.6   CALCULATING INITIAL ALGEBRAS

When we give an algebraic specification, we usually have a specific model in mind that we try to describe. However, there is a fair chance that we have made a mistake somewhere in the specification. This is particularly so for specifications of large and complex systems. The result of most errors is that the initial algebra of the specification at hand does not comply with the model we have in mind.

Tracking down the errors in the specification is facilitated by the use of a tool that generates the initial algebras of the sorts defined in a given specification of data types. This tool only works correctly for a restricted class of specifications, the class of complete term rewriting systems. The initial algebra generator from the PSF-Toolkit, which is called *initial*, tries to calculate a finite projection of the initial algebra for the sorts specified in its TIL input file, by enumerating normal forms. The calculation yields only a finite projection because a lot of specifications deal with infinite sorts, so that calculating their initial algebras would take infinite time. The finiteness of the calculation is guaranteed by specifying an upper bound for the number of elements that an initial algebra may contain. If the program passes this limit it stops generating more normal forms for this sort, and reports this to the user.

An example of the output of *initial* generated for the *decimal numbers* from the PSF Standard Library is given below. The default value (100) for the maximal size of the initial algebras is used in this example and the output has been edited, to cut down its size.

```
*** Initial Algebra Report ***

'DECIMAL': 101 element(s)
*** WARNING : possibly infinite sort. Initial Algebra size reached limit
- (^ 0)
- (^ 1)
- (^ 2)
  ...
- ((^ 9) ^ 9)
- (((^ 1) ^ 0) ^ 0)

'NATURAL': 101 element(s)
*** WARNING : possibly infinite sort. Initial Algebra size reached limit
- zero
- s(zero)
- s(s(zero))
- s(s(s(zero)))
  ...

'BOOLEAN': 2 element(s)
*** WARNING : (in)directly based on possibly infinite sort
- true
- false

'DIGIT': 10 element(s)
```

```
*** WARNING : (in)directly based on possibly infinite sort
 - 0
 - 1
   ...
 - 8
 - 9
```

The warning for the sort *BOOLEAN* is the result of functions which are based on infinite data domains and for which the output type is *BOOLEAN*. An example of such a function is the equality function for *Naturals*.

2.6.7   GENERATING TRANSITION SYSTEMS

We have given specifications of concurrent systems using PSF, but there are other methods for describing processes. One of these somewhat older methods is based on *transition systems*. Transition systems describe a system in terms of a set of *states*, and a set of *labelled transitions* from a *source* state to a *target* state. The labels that are attached to a transition are related to the atomic actions in PSF.

There are algorithms, which are useful for the analysis of processes, that need their input to be in the format of a transition system. A good example of a tool that is based on such an algorithm is the equivalence tester, which we will describe in the next section. Another reason for having a transition system generator in the PSF-Toolkit, is that the *deadlock* and *livelock* properties of a system can be calculated more easily for a transition system than for the equivalent PSF specification.

The term *livelock* is used to describe an *internal infinite loop*. The process is in a state wherein the only possible progress is a cycle of internal actions. Although the process is still active, it will never be able to get out of this cycle.

The main drawbacks of transition systems for use as a specifications language are that it is more difficult to write and to understand a specification in the transition system format and that such specifications tend to be very large. The modelling of parallel execution of two processes leads to an enormous increase of the number of states especially. The reason is that in general, to model the parallel composition of processes *x* and *y*, we have to take the *cartesian product* of the states of *x* and *y* to form a tuple that encodes these new *composite* states. This problem is sometimes referred to as the *state explosion* problem.

The transition system generator is not capable of generating transition systems for every PSF specification. There exist specifications that can be described only by an infinite transition system. Such specifications are rejected by the implementation.

The current implementation of the transition system generator in the PSF-Toolkit is able to handle parameter free process specifications only. However, for small problems it is possible to encode the data information into the names of atomic actions and processes. As an example we apply this procedure to the specification of the boolean memory cell.

```
process module  Boolean-Cell
begin

    atoms
```

```
    read-false, read-true, write-false, write-true

  processes
    Cell, Cell-true, Cell-false

  definitions
    Cell       = read-false . Cell-false + read-true . Cell-true
    Cell-false = write-false . Cell-false + Cell
    Cell-true  = write-true . Cell-true + Cell

  end Boolean-Cell
```

The output of the transition system generator for this example is:

```
Reachable States:

S0  : Cell
S1  : Cell-true
S2  : Cell-false

Transitions for Reachable States:

S0 -(read-false)-> S2
S0 -(read-true)-> S1
S1 -(read-false)-> S2
S1 -(read-true)-> S1
S1 -(write-true)-> S1
S2 -(read-false)-> S2
S2 -(read-true)-> S1
S2 -(write-false)-> S2

... 3 state(s) / 8 transition(s)
```

Besides the feedback to the user, the transition system generator creates a TIL version of the transition system. In this way any program in the PSF-Toolkit that accepts TIL can operate on transition systems.

2.6.8   EQUIVALENCE TESTING

As opposed to the method of proving equality of processes as described in the section on the proof assistant, which was based on interaction between the prover and the proof assistant, there is another fully automated method to verify equality. However, a drawback for this latter method is that it requires transition systems as input. As we have explained in the previous section, these systems can become quite large, even for specifications of moderate size. Furthermore, the input for fully automated equivalence testers is restricted to the class of specifications that can be represented by a finite transition system.

The equivalence tester in the PSF-Toolkit is based on a notion of equality induced by the so-called *branching bisimulation* semantics. The explanation of the notion of *bisimulation* is beyond the scope of this book, but there exist numerous articles on this subject in the literature, to which we refer for detailed information. Whenever two processes are not equal, the equivalence tester generates a formula in the Hennessy-Milner Logic that indicates the difference between both processes.

2.6.9   IMPLEMENTATION & ACKNOWLEDGEMENTS

All programs in the PSF-Toolkit were implemented using the programming language C. Both the simulator and the proof assistant use the X-Windows package to implement a graphical user interface. We would like to thank the following people, in alphabetical order, who contributed to the implementation of the PSF-Toolkit.

D. Barrow implemented a prototype version of the normalizer. B. Diertens wrote the simulator, the proof assistant and the normalizer/type checker. The term rewriter was implemented by C.H.S. Dik. It replaced the Prolog based implementation of the ASF project, which was mainly written by P.R.H. Hendriks. H. Jacobsson contributed to the implementation of the parser. An earlier parser/type checker used the ASF system to carry out type checking of PSF specifications. In this approach a PSF specification is transformed into an ASF specification, such that all typing information is retained. This prototype was written by J.W.C. Koorn. J.C. Mulder implemented the compiler driver and library manager. The equivalence tester was implemented by E.E. Polak. G.J. Veltink contributed to the parser and implemented the transition system generator and initial algebra generator.

2.7   SUMMARY

PSF is a formal specification language suitable for specifying the behaviour of concurrent systems. PSF integrates the process algebra ACP and the algebraic specification language ASF into one language.

PSF specifications consist of two kind of modules: data modules, which describe data types, and process modules, which describe process behaviour. Atomic actions and processes can be parameterized with data. The language PSF incorporates several modularization concepts such as exports, imports and parameters.

The PSF-Toolkit is a set of computer programs that form a programming environment for PSF. The available tools are: a compiler, a term rewriter, a simulator, a proof assistant, an initial algebra generator, an equivalence tester and a transition system generator. Besides the above-mentioned tools, the PSF environment contains the PSF Standard Library. The PSF Standard Library implements a set of frequently used data types.

Some aspects of communication protocols cannot be modeled with PSF, such as time dependent behaviour. Although it is possible to specify protocols that are robust with respect to premature time-outs, protocols of which the correct behaviour depends on the adjustment of a timer cannot be described. However, extensions of the theory ACP contain special operators which deal with real-time or priorities between actions.

2.8 BIBLIOGRAPHICAL NOTES

For information about the mathematical foundation of ACP we refer to [BW90]. The collected volume [Bae90] contains examples of applications of ACP. In this book ACP is applied systematically to a number of situations, including systolic algorithms, semantics of an object oriented language, and verification of protocols. The paper in which ACP was introduced is [BK84].

Information about CCS can be found in [Mil89] and for CSP we refer to [Hoa85]. For the definition of ASF and further information about the language we refer to [BHK89].

The notion of bisimulation was first described in [Par81] and the action relations we use to define the operational semantics were first used in [Plo82]. The Hennessy-Milner Logic is defined in [HM85]. An algorithm for deciding branching bisimulation can be found in [GV90], and the extension to this algorithm to generate distinguishing formulae is given in [Kor92].

For more information about initial algebras and other semantics for equational specifications we refer to [EM85] and [GM85].

Information about the language PSF and proposed extensions can be found in [Mau91]. The definition of the language PSF is [MV90], a different introduction to the language can be found in [MV89a]. The language TIL is described in both [Mau91] and [MV89b]. For a detailed description of the translation from PSF to TIL, and for the definition of M-TIL and I-TIL we refer to [Vel90].

There are several other specification languages that are supported by a computer environment. One of the languages that is quite similar to PSF is LOTOS. The definition of LOTOS is [ISO89], a tutorial is [BB87]. Two specification languages that that have been implemented by means of implementing a different front-end to the PSF-Toolkit are μCRL [GP90] and XP [Vel91].

The term rewriter in the PSF-Toolkit is based on the system described in [Dik89]. For more general information about implementations of term rewriting systems we refer to [Kap87]. The proof assistant in the PSF-Toolkit is described in more detail in [MV92]. A very similar tool has been developed in the CCS setting [Lin92].

The equivalence tester in the PSF-Toolkit is described in [Pol92]. A description of a tool set for deciding a larger class of equivalences can be found in [FM91].

Descriptions of sets of computer tools for formalisms different from PSF are the Concurrency Workbench [CPS89] which is based on CCS, LITE the LOTOSPHERE Integrated Tool Environment which is described in [Eij91] and the AUTO system [Ver91] which supports specifications based on the theory of automata.

CHAPTER 3
SIMPLE PROTOCOLS

J.J. VAN WAMEL

3.1 INTRODUCTION

In this chapter specifications of three simple protocols are given in the formalism of
PSF. The main goal is to make the reader familiar with the way the formal
description technique PSF can be used for the specification of communication
protocols. For this reason we specify protocols which are, in technical terms, not
hard to understand.

The communication protocols specified in this chapter are the Alternating Bit
Protocol (ABP), the Positive Acknowledgement with Retransmission Protocol (PAR-
Protocol), and the Concurrent Alternating Bit Protocol (CABP), which is a more
complicated version of the ABP.

The three protocols have in common that they follow a simplex scheme, which
means that there is only one sender and one receiver and that the data flows in one
direction. Moreover, the protocols handle just one data element at a time. These two
restrictions make the protocols behave externally as one-element buffers.

The simple protocols considered have an interesting history in the theories of
concurrency. Many different specifications and verifications can be found in the
literature. Our specifications of the simple protocols are based on existing specifications in ACP that were made for mathematical analysis.

The ABP as specified in this chapter has been verified algebraically in the
formalism of ACP. The PAR-Protocol has also been specified and verified by means
of ACP but a special operator was needed to specify some restrictions on the
communication between the timer process and the sender process: the priority
operator. We present a version without priorities which is very similar to this
specification. This is because priorities cannot be specified in PSF.

Section 3.2 gives a description of some general aspects of the simple protocols. Similarities between the protocols are sketched and some remarks are made on the internal and external behaviour of the simple protocols. Also a criterion for the correctness of the protocols is formulated.

Section 3.3 gives a description and a full specification of the ABP in PSF. In a similar way, the PAR-Protocol and the CABP are described and specified in sections 3.4 and 3.5 respectively.

3.2 GENERAL DESCRIPTION

We will only consider protocols that manage the communication between two external users. They follow a so-called simplex scheme as described in chapter 1 of this book: one of these users communicates data to a sender at an input port. The other takes it from a receiver at an output port. These input and output actions are considered the external behaviour of a simple protocol.

All actions that happen between the input action and the output action are the internal actions of the protocol. Internal actions take place for instance in the channels which connect the sender and the receiver; the channels make internal decisions whether to send data correctly, to corrupt it or to loose it. Other examples of internal actions are the transmission of data from the sender to a channel, and the transmission of data from a channel to the receiver.

In general terms, correct (external) behaviour of the simple protocols can be formulated as follows: each data element that is read by the sender has to be transmitted to the output port exactly once. In order to achieve this, the data elements are labelled with the two-valued bits as control data. The combination of a data element with a bit will be called a frame. For acknowledgements bits are used or a constant message. The right order of the transmission of data elements is automatically preserved in these protocols because the sender only accepts a new data element after the old one has been acknowledged and transmitted correctly.

We can mention a few characteristics of correct simple protocol behaviour. The receiver must be sure that the received data element has not been corrupted during transmission before it is passed through to the output. We will suppose that this is achieved by the computation of a checksum. The computation of this checksum provides the receiver with the means to decide whether data has been transmitted correctly or not. If the receiver receives a checksum error it sends either an error message to the sender, implicitly asking for a retransmission of the garbled data element, or it just waits for a retransmission initiated by a time-out at the sender. Correct data elements are passed through to the output and an acknowledgement is sent to the sender. After reception of a correct acknowledgement, the next data element can be read at the input.

The correct behaviour of many protocols, for instance the ABP, depends on a restriction on the channels; no messages must get lost during their trip through the channel. But a protocol may also take into account the possibility of data elements getting totally lost in a channel. We suppose that the communication channels satisfy the requirement of fairness such that sooner or later a non-corrupted data element arrives at the receiver. We will see two different mechanisms for handling

the possible loss of data elements in a channel. In the PAR-Protocol a timer is added
to the sender. If after some time no acknowledgement has arrived, a retransmission of
the lost data element is initiated by a time-out. In the CABP, no timer processes are
needed to overcome the loss of data in the channels. The sender of the CABP just
keeps firing a data element into the channel until it is acknowledged. In this
protocol, acknowledgements are also sent in a continuous stream to the sender.

As mentioned above, the protocols specified in this chapter follow a simple
read/send scheme. The reading of data elements is done by a sender at the input port,
the sending of data elements is done by a receiver at the output port. Furthermore,
after a data element is read, the only possible external action is the sending of this
data element. So the protocol behaves externally as a one-element buffer. The
components and ports of the simple protocols can be represented schematically as in
Figure 3.1. The small boxes represent the separate components of the system such as
the sender, the receiver and the channels. The arrows indicate the ports through
which the communication between the components takes place and the direction in
which the data flows. The channel between the sender and the receiver is split into
two separate channels K and L because we assume the data stream from the sender to
the receiver not to interfere with the acknowledgement stream in the opposite
direction.

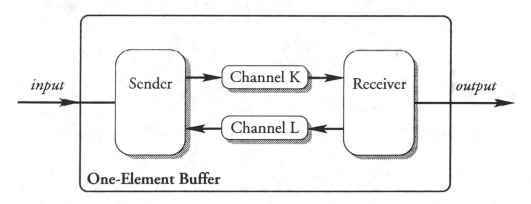

Figure 3.1   Components and ports of the Simple Protocols

The PSF specification of a one-element buffer *Buf* is given below. The data module
Data is specified in the PSF standard library. It contains a parameter that must be
bound to the actual data to be transmitted.

```
process module  One-Element-Buffer
begin

   exports
     begin
       atoms
         r1, s2 : DATA
```

```
     processes
        Buf
     end

  imports
     Data

  definitions
     Buf = sum( d in DATA, r1(d).s2(d).Buf )

  end One-Element-Buffer
```

Now it is easy to formulate the external behaviour of a given specification of a simple protocol. After abstraction from the internal actions a simple protocol behaves as *Buf*. Of the protocols specified in this chapter, only the CABP has the possibility of starting with some sequence of internal actions. So the CABP behaves as a buffer that can also start with such a sequence.

Below, we present some definitions that are used throughout the specifications in this chapter:

d	data element from a finite data set $DATA$ (see the PSF standard library)
$datum$	element from a generalised data set TD containing all transferable data including the set $DATA$
P	the set of port numbers
p	an element from the port set P
$p = 1$	input port
$p = 2$	output port
$rp(datum)$	read datum at port p
$sp(datum)$	send datum at port p
$cp(datum)$	communicate datum at port p $rp(datum) \mid sp(datum) = cp(datum)$

3.3 ALTERNATING BIT PROTOCOL

One of the simplest communication protocols is the Alternating Bit Protocol. The ABP is a well known example from concurrency theory because it is often used as a first test-case for new (extensions of) theories.

3.3.1   DESCRIPTION OF THE ABP

In this section the operational behaviour of the Alternating Bit Protocol is described. The processes and ports of the ABP are depicted in Figure 3.2. In addition, the data that can be communicated through the ports is shown. The numbers *1,..., 6* represent the port numbers, *b* is a bit and *1-b* is its inverse.

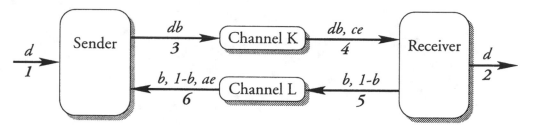

Figure 3.2   Processes and ports of the ABP

The sender S starts by reading a data element d at port 1. Then a frame consisting of the data element and a control bit b is sent via channel K to the receiver R. If R receives a frame, the checksum is computed and the control bit is checked. The procedure of the reception of a frame and the computation of the checksum at the receiver is modelled as a non-deterministic choice of the channel between the transmission of a frame or a checksum error. The channels can not loose data or generate new data. If the received frame is the expected frame (control bit b) and the checksum is correct, the data element is sent at port 2 and an acknowledgement b is sent into channel L. Otherwise an acknowledgement $1-b$ is sent into channel L. If a correct acknowledgement b arrives at S via channel L a new data element is read at the input and the procedure is repeated with the control bit inverted. Otherwise the old frame is retransmitted. The errors the channels may produce are the following:

ce :   checksum error that can be detected by the receiver.
ae :   acknowledgement error that can be detected by the sender.

The channels K and L can contain only one datum. This can be understood easily: if the sender has sent a frame it waits for a message from the receiver which is only sent after reception of this frame or a checksum error. Similarly, the receiver just awaits the arrival of a frame after it has sent a message.

3.3.2   SPECIFICATION OF THE ABP IN PSF

With the process modules of PSF the modular structure of the protocol can be preserved: one process module per component. One data module has to be introduced, which is for the specification of the frames.

3.3.2.1 Frames

Frames is the only data module we have to specify for the ABP. It imports two data modules from the PSF standard library: *Bits* and *Data*. Each component of the ABP consists of processes parameterized with data so each process module imports the data module *Frames*.

```
data module Frames
begin

   exports
     begin
```

```
      sorts
        FRAME, ERROR
      functions
        frame : DATA # BIT -> FRAME
        ce    :              -> ERROR
        ae    :              -> ERROR
   end

 imports
    Bits, Data

end Frames
```

3.3.2.2 Sender

The module *Sender* specifies the sender process *S* of the ABP. *S* is initialized with
bit0. The constant *bit0* as well as the function *invert* are specified in the module *Bits*.
The sender reads a data element *d* at *port 1*, adds a control bit *b* and communicates
frame(d,b) to channel *K*. After the reception of *b* from channel *L* the procedure is
repeated from the start with bit *1-b*. The reception of a garbled acknowledgement *ae*
from channel *L* leads to a retransmission of *frame(d,b)*. The reception of *1-b* indicates
the reception of a checksum error by the receiver. In this case the frame also has to be
retransmitted. The names used for the processes are the following:

RM :   Read a Message (data element) at the input port
SF :   Send a Frame into channel *K*
RA :   Receive an Acknowledgement from channel *L*

```
process module  Sender
begin

  exports
    begin
      atoms
        r1 : DATA
        s3 : FRAME
        r6 : BIT
        r6 : ERROR
      processes
        S
    end

  imports
    Frames

  processes
    RM : BIT
    SF : FRAME
    RA : FRAME

  variables
    d : -> DATA
    b : -> BIT
```

```
definitions
  S = RM(bit0)
  RM(b) = sum( d in DATA, r1(d) . SF(frame(d,b)) )
  SF(frame(d,b)) = s3(frame(d,b)) . RA(frame(d,b))
  RA(frame(d,b)) = ( r6(invert(b)) + r6(ae) ) . SF(frame(d,b))
       + r6(b) . RM(invert(b))

end Sender
```

3.3.2.3 Message Channel

The messages from the sender to the receiver are transported through channel K. Channel K can communicate a correct frame or a checksum error at *port 4*. The choice between these two alternatives is made non-deterministically, which is achieved by the use of *skips*.

```
process module  Channel-K
begin

  exports
    begin
      atoms
        r3, s4   : FRAME
        s4       : ERROR
      processes
        K
    end

  imports
    Frames

  processes
    K : FRAME

  variables
    f : -> FRAME

  definitions
    K = sum( f in FRAME, r3(f) . K(f) )
    K(f) = ( skip . s4(f) + skip . s4(ce) ) . K

end Channel-K
```

3.3.2.4 Receiver

The module *Receiver* specifies the receiver process R of the ABP. Just as the sender, the receiver is initialized with *bit0*. After a correct frame *frame(d,b)* is received, the data element d is sent at the output port and an acknowledgement b is communicated to channel L. After the reception of a checksum error an acknowledgement *1-b* is communicated to channel L.

  RF : Receive a Frame from channel K
  SM : Send a Message (data element) at the output port
  SA : Send an Acknowledgement into channel L

```
process module  Receiver
begin

  exports
    begin
      atoms
        r4 : FRAME
        r4 : ERROR
        s2 : DATA
        s5 : BIT
      processes
        R
    end

  imports
    Frames

  processes
    RF : BIT
    SM : FRAME
    SA : BIT

  variables
    d : -> DATA
    b : -> BIT

  definitions
    R = RF(bit0)
    RF(b) = sum( d in DATA, r4(frame(d,b)) . SM(frame(d,b)) )
        +  sum( d in DATA, r4(frame(d,invert(b))) . SA(invert(b)) )
        +  r4(ce) . SA(invert(b)
    SA(b) = s5(b) . RF(invert(b))
    SM(frame(d,b)) = s2(d) . SA(b)

end Receiver
```

3.3.2.5 Acknowledgement Channel

The messages from the sender to the receiver are transported through channel L. Channel L can communicate a correct acknowledgement or an acknowledgement error at *port 6*. The choice between these two alternatives is made non-deterministically, as in channel K.

```
process module  Channel-L
begin

  exports
    begin
      atoms
        r5, s6  : BIT
        s6      : ERROR
      processes
        L
    end
```

```
    imports
      Frames

    processes
      L : BIT

    variables
      b : -> BIT

    definitions
      L = sum( b in BIT, r5(b) . L(b) )
      L(b) = ( skip . s6(b) + skip . s6(ae) ) . L

  end Channel-L
```

3.3.2.6 ABP

The top module *ABP* is the process module which imports the four separate
components and makes the specification of the protocol complete. The encapsulation
set and the communications are defined and the process *ABP* is defined as the
parallel composition of the components.

```
  process module ABP
  begin

    exports
      begin
        atoms
          c3, c4 : FRAME
          c5, c6 : BIT
          c4, c6 : ERROR
        processes
          ABP
      end

    imports
      Sender, Channel-K, Receiver, Channel-L

    sets
      of atoms
        H = {r3(f), s3(f), r4(f), s4(f) | f in FRAME}
          + {r5(b), s5(b), r6(b), s6(b) | b in BIT}
          + {r4(e), s4(e), r6(e), s6(e) | e in ERROR}

    communications
      s3(f) | r3(f) = c3(f)   for f in FRAME
      s4(f) | r4(f) = c4(f)   for f in FRAME
      s5(b) | r5(b) = c5(b)   for b in BIT
      s6(b) | r6(b) = c6(b)   for b in BIT
      s4(e) | r4(e) = c4(e)   for e in ERROR
      s6(e) | r6(e) = c6(e)   for e in ERROR
    definitions
      ABP = encaps( H, S || K || R || L )

  end ABP
```

3.3.2.7 Simulation of the ABP

Below, we give a trace through the state space of the specification above as generated by the PSF simulator. The transmission of two data elements is shown. The first transmission is error free and in the second transmission the protocol has to deal with a checksum error.

```
atom  r1(d3)                    -- data element d3 is read by the sender
com.  c3(frame(d3, bit0))
      skip
com.  c4(frame(d3, bit0))
atom  s2(d3)                    -- data element d3 is sent by the receiver
com.  c5(bit0)
      skip
com.  c6(bit0)          -- the transmission of d3 is completed error free
atom  r1(d2)                    -- data element d2 is read by the sender
com.  c3(frame(d2, bit1))
      skip
com.  c4(ce)                -- a checksum error arrives at the receiver
com.  c5(bit0)
      skip
com.  c6(bit0)        -- the sender is informed about the checksum error
com.  c3(frame(d2, bit1))        -- the frame with d2 is sent again
      skip
com.  c4(frame(d2, bit1))
atom  s2(d2)                    -- data element d2 is sent by the receiver
com.  c5(bit1)
      skip
com.  c6(bit1)                  -- the transmission of d1 is completed
```

3.3.2.8 Remark on the Specification of the Channels.

It is sometimes a complicated technical problem to predict how a change in the capacity of the channels influences the behaviour of the protocol. In some protocols changes occur in the external behaviour, in some only the internal behaviour changes, and in others nothing changes. It was argued that the channels in the ABP can contain only one datum at a time. This can be regarded a characteristic of the protocol. A consequence of this fact is that the channels can be replaced by queues of arbitrary capacity without affecting the internal behaviour of the protocol. These queues must have the same properties as the channels K and L, of course, such as the non-deterministic choice between correct and faulty transmission.

3.4   Positive Acknowledgement with Retransmission Protocol

The Positive Acknowledgement with Retransmission Protocol is quite similar to the ABP in the sense that, if the sender or the receiver has sent a message, it waits for a reaction from the receiver or sender respectively. The main difference can be described as follows: the PAR-Protocol takes the possibility into account of data getting lost in one of the channels. The ABP will get stuck if a message gets lost because both the sender and the receiver will get in a state of just waiting for something to happen. A solution to this problem is the addition of a timer to the sender which is started as soon as a frame is sent into channel K. If a message now gets lost, after some time a time-out signal is sent to the sender and a retransmission follows. Other differences are that the PAR-protocol uses a constant for acknowledgements, and that the receiver only sends an acknowledgement into channel L after the expected frame has arrived. This single-valued acknowledgement explains 'Positive Acknowledgement' in the name of the protocol.

3.4.1   DESCRIPTION OF THE PAR-PROTOCOL

An important characteristic of the PAR-Protocol is that an additional ACP operator is needed to guarantee correct behaviour: the priority operator. The difficulty is that each time a frame is sent the timer is started. A time-out can then occur in every state of the system.

We will sketch one sequence of events that will make the protocol fail if we allow premature time-outs. If a time-out occurs when an acknowledgement is still on its way, the acknowledged frame is retransmitted. The acknowledgement arrives and the sender reads a new data element. The receiver meanwhile receives the old frame and sends an acknowledgement back. Now, the new frame can get lost while an acknowledgement arrives at the sender. A third frame is read at the input and the second frame simply disappears. The priority operator prevents such premature time-outs by only allowing them to occur when nothing else can happen. This is the case when both sender and receiver are waiting.

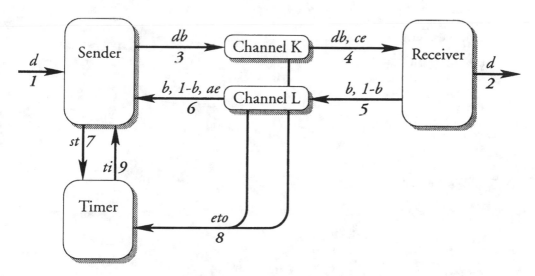

Figure 3.3   Processes and ports of the PAR-Protocol

See Figure 3.3 for the processes and ports of the PAR-Protocol. The signal *st* starts the timer, the signal *eto* enables the timer to generate a time-out and *ti* is the time-out signal. The connections between the channels and the timer process will be explained below.

We will give an alternative specification without the priority operator. If a datum gets lost in one of the channels or if a checksum error arrives at the receiver, a time-out is supposed to occur after some time at the sender. The channels 'cause' a time-out. We model this causal relation by enabling the timer in these cases to send a time-out to the sender. The timer is started after a data element is read by the sender. After this, the frame with the data element is immediately sent into channel *K*.

As in the ABP, the channels can be replaced by queues with arbitrary capacity without changing the internal behaviour of the protocol.

3.4.2   SPECIFICATION OF THE PAR-PROTOCOL IN PSF

As in the specification of the ABP, we start with the specification of the data. After that, the process modules are specified. Note the similarity between the specification of the ABP and the specification of the PAR-Protocol.

3.4.2.1 Frames

The module *Frames* imports *Bits* and *Data* from the PSF standard library. An extra data module *Timer-Signals* is used to specify the timer signals.

```
data module Frames
begin

  exports
    begin
      sorts
        FRAME, ERROR, ACK
      functions
        frame   : DATA # BIT  -> FRAME
        ce      :             -> ERROR
        ae      :             -> ERROR
        ac      :             -> ACK
    end

  imports
    Bits, Data

end Frames



data module Timer-Signals
begin

  exports
    begin
      sorts
        TIMER-SIGNAL
      functions
        st    : -> TIMER-SIGNAL
        ti    : -> TIMER-SIGNAL
        eto   : -> TIMER-SIGNAL
    end
end Timer-Signals
```

3.4.2.2 Sender

The PAR-Protocol is also initialized with *bit0*. The process names of the sender are chosen to be quite similar to those of the ABP sender. The sender first reads a data element *d* at *port 1*, then the timer is started and a control bit *b* is added to the data element, and *frame(d,b)* is communicated to channel *K*. If after this an acknowledgement *ac* is received from channel *L*, the procedure is repeated with the control bit inverted. After a time-out or after the reception of a garbled acknowledgement *ae* the old frame is sent again.

ST : Start the Timer

RM, SF and RA : see the ABP specification

```
process module  Sender
begin

    exports
      begin
        atoms
            r1        : DATA
            s3        : FRAME
            r6        : ACK
            r6        : ERROR
            s7, r9    : TIMER-SIGNAL

        processes
            S

      end
    imports
      Frames, Timer-Signals

    processes
      RM : BIT
      ST : FRAME
      SF : FRAME
      RA : FRAME

    variables
      d : -> DATA
      b : -> BIT

    definitions
      S = RM(bit0)
      RM(b) = sum( d in DATA, r1(d) . ST(frame(d,b)) )
      ST(frame(d,b)) = s7(st) . SF(frame(d,b))
      SF(frame(d,b)) = s3(frame(d,b)) . RA(frame(d,b))
      RA(frame(d,b)) = ( r9(ti) + r6(ae) ) . ST(frame(d,b))
            + r6(ac) . RM(invert(b))

end Sender
```

3.4.2.3 Timer

When the timer is running it can receive another start signal *st* or an enable time-out signal *eto*. When the timer is enabled it can send a time-out signal *ti* to the sender. No start signal can be expected in this state because both the sender and the receiver are waiting for a message and the channels are empty. The timer is specified with three processes:

T :   inactive Timer

TR :   the Timer is Running

TE :   the Timer is Enabled to send a time-out to the sender

```
process module  Timer
begin

  exports
    begin
      atoms
        r7, r8, s9 : TIMER-SIGNAL
      processes
        T
    end

  imports
    Timer-Signals

  processes
    TR, TE

  definitions
    T = r7(st) . TR
    TR = r7(st) . TR + r8(eto) . TE
    TE = s9(ti) . T

end Timer
```

3.4.2.4 Message Channel

In channel K there are three alternatives between which a non-deterministic choice is made. After the loss of a frame or the transmission of a checksum error, the timer needs to be enabled to generate a time-out. This causal relation is modelled with the sending of an *eto* signal.

```
process module  Channel-K
begin

  exports
    begin
      atoms
        r3, s4  : FRAME
        s4      : ERROR
      processes
        K
    end
```

```
imports
   Frames, Channel-L

processes
   K1 : FRAME
   K2

variables
   f : -> FRAME

definitions
   K = sum( f in FRAME, r3(f) . K1(f) )
   K1(f) = ( skip + skip . s4(ce) ) . K2 + skip . s4(f) . K
   K2 = s8(eto) . K

end Channel-K
```

3.4.2.5 Receiver

The process names in the specification of the receiver are chosen to be similar to those of the ABP receiver. If the receiver receives a correct frame, the data element from this frame is sent at the output port and an acknowledgement *ac* is sent into channel *L*. If a checksum error arrives the receiver simply starts waiting again for a frame because a time-out at the sender will lead to retransmission of the garbled frame. The reception of a frame with the wrong control bit (an old frame) also has to be acknowledged because the sender will not read a new data element before an acknowledgement arrives.

```
process module Receiver
begin

   exports
     begin
       atoms
           r4 : FRAME
           r4 : ERROR
           s2 : DATA
           s5 : ACK
       processes
           R
     end

   imports
       Frames

   processes
       RF : BIT
       SM : FRAME
       SA : BIT

   variables
       d : -> DATA
       b : -> BIT
```

```
definitions
  R = RF(bit0)
  RF(b) = sum( d in DATA, r4(frame(d,b)) . SM(frame(d,b)) )
        + sum( d in DATA, r4(frame(d,invert(b))) . SA(b) )
        + r4(ce) . RF(b)
  SA(b) = s5(ac) . RF(b)
  SM(frame(d,b)) = s2(d) . SA(invert(b))

end Receiver
```

3.4.2.6   Acknowledgement Channel

The structure of channel L is quite similar to that of channel K. One difference is that now only the loss of a message can lead to a time-out.

```
process module  Channel-L
begin

    exports
      begin
        atoms
          r5, s6  : ACK
          s6      : ERROR
          s8      : TIMER-SIGNAL
        processes
          L
      end

    imports
      Frames, Timer-Signals

    processes
      L1, L2

    definitions
      L = r5(ac) . L1
      L1 = ( skip . s6(ae) + skip . s6(ac) ) . L + skip . L2
      L2 = s8(eto) . L

end Channel-L
```

3.4.2.7   PAR

The top module PAR defines the PAR-Protocol, in the form of the process PAR, as the parallel composition of the five components specified above.

```
process module  PAR
begin

    exports
      begin
        atoms
          c3, c4     : FRAME
          c5, c6     : ACK
          c4, c6     : ERROR
          c7, c8, c9 : TIMER-SIGNAL
```

```
      processes
         PAR
   end

imports
   Sender, Timer, Channel-K, Receiver, Channel-L

sets
   of  atoms
      H = {r3(f), s3(f), r4(f), s4(f) | f in FRAME}
        + {r4(e), s4(e), r6(e), s6(e) | e in ERROR}
        + {r5(ac), s5(ac), r6(ac), s6(ac)}
        + {r7(st), s7(st), r8(eto), s8(eto), r9(ti), s9(ti)}

communications
   s4(e) | r4(e) = c4(e)      for e in ERROR
   s6(e) | r6(e) = c6(e)      for e in ERROR
   s3(f) | r3(f) = c3(f)      for f in FRAME
   s4(f) | r4(f) = c4(f)      for f in FRAME
   s5(ac) | r5(ac) = c5(ac)
   s6(ac) | r6(ac) = c6(ac)
   s7(st) | r7(st) = c7(st)
   s9(ti) | r9(ti) = c9(ti)
   s8(eto) | r8(eto) = c8(eto)

definitions
   PAR = encaps( H, S || K || R || L || T )

end  PAR
```

3.5   CONCURRENT ALTERNATING BIT PROTOCOL

The Concurrent Alternating Bit Protocol is a more complicated variant of the ABP. This protocol can be active at more than one communication port at the same time. This is why it is called 'Concurrent'. It is described and specified in this section.

3.5.1   DESCRIPTION OF THE CABP

The differences between the CABP and the ABP can be stated as follows: the sender is split into two components. One component, the sending part, does the reading from the input port and sends a continuous stream of frames into channel K and the other component handles incoming acknowledgements.

The receiver is also split into two components. One component, the receiving part, receives frames from channel K and takes care of the output port. The other component, the acknowledgement sender, fires a continuous stream of acknowledgements into channel L.

This continuous retransmission of frames and acknowledgements makes it possible to deal with channels that can loose data. Especially in cases where the data takes a long time to travel through the channels this protocol can be more efficient than the ABP and the PAR-protocol. This will depend on the retransmission rates of both frames and acknowledgements. Figure 3.4 gives the processes and ports of the CABP.

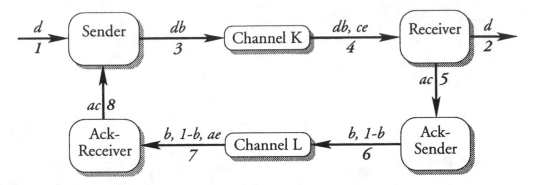

Figure 3.4   Processes and ports of the CABP

One can imagine that the channels in the CABP might contain more than one datum. Replacing the channels by queues with capacity greater than one will change the internal behaviour and increase the state space.

3.5.2   SPECIFICATION OF THE CABP IN PSF

3.5.2.1   Frames
The data module *Frames* of the CABP is very similar to the data module *Frames* of the ABP. Only a constant *ac* of the sort *ACK* is added. This constant *ac* serves as the acknowledgement communicated at ports 5 and 8.

```
data module  Frames
begin

  exports
    begin
      sorts
        FRAME, ERROR, ACK
      functions
        frame : DATA # BIT -> FRAME
        ce    :            -> ERROR
        ae    :            -> ERROR
        ac    :            -> ACK
    end

  imports
    Bits, Data

end Frames
```

3.5.2.2 Sender

The sender and receiver processes of the CABP are, just as those of the other two protocols, initialized with the parameter *bit0*. The sender reads a data element *d* at *port 1* and adds a control bit *b*. Then a continuous stream of frames *frame(d,b)* is communicated to channel *K* until an acknowledgement *ac* arrives from the acknowledgement receiver. After the reception of *ac*, a new data element is read at the input port and the control bit is inverted.

```
process module  Sender
begin

    exports
      begin
        atoms
          r1 : DATA
          s3 : FRAME
          r8 : ACK
        processes
          S
      end

    imports
      Frames

    processes
      RM : BIT
      SF : FRAME

    variables
      d : -> DATA
      b : -> BIT

    definitions
      S = RM(bit0)
      RM(b) = sum( d in DATA, r1(d) . SF(frame(d,b)) )
      SF(frame(d,b)) = s3(frame(d,b)) . SF(frame(d,b))
          + r8(ac) . RM(invert(b))

end Sender
```

3.5.2.3 Message Channel

Channel *K* is the message channel of the ABP with one choice option added: a simple *skip*, which denotes the loss of a frame.

```
process module  Channel-K
begin

    exports
      begin
        atoms
          r3, s4  : FRAME
          s4      : ERROR
```

```
      processes
         K
      end

   imports
     Frames

   processes
     K : FRAME

   variables
     f : -> FRAME

   definitions
     K = sum( f in FRAME, r3(f) . K(f) )
     K(f) = ( skip . s4(f) + skip . s4(ce) + skip ) . K

  end Channel-K
```

3.5.2.4 Receiver

If a correct frame arrives the receiver first sends the data element at the output port, and then it sends an acknowledgement to the acknowledgement sender. Note that the receiver of the CABP, just as the receiver of the PAR-Protocol, does not take any notice of the reception of checksum errors.

```
  process module Receiver
  begin

    exports
      begin
        atoms
          r4 : FRAME
          r4 : ERROR
          s2 : DATA
          s5 : ACK
        processes
          R
      end

    imports
      Frames

    processes
      RF : BIT

    variables
      d : -> DATA
      b : -> BIT

    definitions
      R = RF(bit0)
      RF(b) = sum( d in DATA,
                   r4(frame(d,b)) . s2(d) . s5(ac) . RF(invert(b)) )
            + sum( d in DATA, r4(frame(d,invert(b))) . RF(b) )
```

```
        +   r4(ce)  .  RF(b)

    end Receiver
```

3.5.2.5 Acknowledgement Sender

The acknowledgement sender *AS* is initialized with *bit1*. This is because the first frame that is to be transmitted must not be acknowledged before it has been arrived correctly at the receiver. The acknowledgement receiver sends a continuous stream of bits into channel *L*.

```
process module  Ack-Sender
begin

  exports
    begin
      atoms
        r5 : ACK
        s6 : BIT
      processes
        AS
    end

  imports
    Frames

  processes
    AS : BIT

  variables
    b : -> BIT

  definitions
    AS = AS(bit1)
    AS(b) = r5(ac) . AS(invert(b)) + s6(b) . AS(b)

end Ack-Sender
```

3.5.2.6 Acknowledgement Channel

Channel *L* is obtained from the acknowledgement channel of the ABP by adding a *skip* as an extra alternative and by changing the port numbers.

```
process module  Channel-L
begin

  exports
    begin
      atoms
        r6, s7  : BIT
        s7      : ERROR
      processes
        L
    end
```

```
    imports
      Frames

    processes
      L : BIT

    variables
      b : -> BIT

    definitions
      L = sum( b in BIT, r6(b) . L(b) )
      L(b) = ( skip . s7(b) + skip . s7(ae) + skip ) . L

  end Channel-L
```

3.5.2.7 Acknowledgement Receiver

The acknowledgement receiver *AR* is initialized with *bit0*. The acknowledgement sender was initialized with *bit1*. Therefore, as long as this *bit1* is received by the acknowledgement receiver, no acknowledgement is sent to the sender. After an acknowledgement has been sent, the value of the expected bit is inverted.

```
    process module Ack-Receiver
    begin

      exports
        begin
          atoms
            r7 : ERROR
            r7 : BIT
            s8 : ACK
          processes
            AR
        end

      imports
        Frames

      processes
        AR : BIT

      variables
        b : -> BIT

      definitions
        AR = AR(bit0)
        AR(b) = ( r7(ae) + r7(invert(b)) ) . AR(b)
            + r7(b) . s8(ac) . AR(invert(b))

    end Ack-Receiver
```

3.5.2.8 CABP

In the top module *CABP* the process *CABP* is defined as the parallel composition of the six components defined above.

```
process module CABP
begin

   exports
     begin
       atoms
         c3, c4 : FRAME
         c5, c8 : ACK
         c6, c7 : BIT
         c4, c7 : ERROR
       processes
         CABP
     end

   imports
     Sender, Channel-K, Receiver, Channel-L, Ack-Sender, Ack-Receiver

   sets
     of atoms
       H = {r3(f), s3(f), r4(f), s4(f) | f in FRAME}
         + {r5(ac), s5(ac), r8(ac), s8(ac)}
         + {r6(b), s6(b), r7(b), s7(b) | b in BIT}
         + {r4(e), s4(e), r7(e), s7(e) | c in ERROR}

   communications
       s3(f) | r3(f) = c3(f)    for f in FRAME
       s4(f) | r4(f) = c4(f)    for f in FRAME
       s5(ac) | r5(ac) = c5(ac)
       s8(ac) | r8(ac) = c8(ac)
       s6(b) | r6(b) = c6(b)    for b in BIT
       s7(b) | r7(b) = c7(b)    for b in BIT
       s4(e) | r4(e) = c4(e)    for e in ERROR
       s7(e) | r7(e) = c7(e)    for e in ERROR

   definitions
       CABP = encaps( H, S || K || R || AS || L || AR )

end CABP
```

3.6 SUMMARY

Three simple protocols were specified in PSF. It should be clear from these specifications that the modular structure of PSF supports the component-wise specification of communication protocols in separate process modules.

All data that plays a role in a protocol, as well as functions on this data, can be specified in data modules. For each simple protocol a module *Frames* was specified, which in its turn imported the modules *Bits* and *Data* from the standard library of PSF. The PAR-Protocol needed one extra data module, *Timer-Signals*, for the specification of the signals to and from the timer. The only function that was used in the specifications is the function *invert*, which is defined on the bits.

3.7 BIBLIOGRAPHICAL NOTES

For a specification and verification of the ABP in ACP the reader is referred to [Vaa90] or [BW90].

The PAR-Protocol with the priority mechanism is specified and verified in [Vaa90]. It can be proved that our specification is identical to the specification in [Vaa90] in branching bisimulation semantics after abstraction from the communication actions between the sender and timer processes.

The ACP specification of the CABP we presented was given in [KM90]. In the same paper a verification based on bisimulation techniques can be found. An algebraic verification of this protocol can be found in [Wam92a]. In [GV89] a specification and verification of a CABP is given with channels that behave as FIFO-queues with unbounded capacity that can loose data.

An interesting example of how the capacity of the communication channels can influence the external behaviour of a protocol can be found in [Wam92b].

CHAPTER 4
SLIDING WINDOW PROTOCOLS

J.J. BRUNEKREEF

4.1 INTRODUCTION

Sliding Window Protocols are used to provide reliable data communication between two computers in a network environment. A Sliding Window Protocol is *connection oriented*: a logical connection between the computers is established before data are transferred. Establishing a connection is not part of a Sliding Window Protocol. The connection is supposed to be a *point-to-point* connection without an intermediate network station. Sliding Window Protocols are situated in the Data Link Layer of the ISO OSI layer model.

In Tanenbaum ([Tan89]) three Sliding Window Protocols are presented. In this chapter a formal specification of these protocols is given. In the remainder of this section we give a general and informal description of a Sliding Window Protocol. In sections 4.2 to 4.4 the different Sliding Window Protocols are introduced and specified in PSF. The communication between Host processes and a Sliding Window Protocol is specified in section 4.5.

4.1.1 GENERAL DESCRIPTION OF A SLIDING WINDOW PROTOCOL

A Sliding Window Protocol (SWP) manages the communication on a point-to-point connection between two computers in a network at the Data Link Layer level in the OSI terminology. A SWP is a full-duplex protocol. This means that data can be transmitted simultaneously from station A to station B and vice versa. On both sides a SWP process is active, taking care of correct transmission. A SWP process contains a sending and a receiving part, managing outgoing and incoming data respectively. As we shall see in the sequel, these parts are not fully separated.

Before transmission a stream of data is split into *packets* of a certain size. The SWP supposes that a host delivers a continuous stream of these data packets. The time between the deliverance of two packets may vary from 'very short' to 'very long'. The SWP has to deliver the packets to another host in the same order as the order in which they were delivered to the SWP.

In order to achieve a correct transmission the SWP expands a data packet to a *data frame*. A frame consists of a data packet with additional fields. A first field contains a *frame number*, by which a receiving station can check the order in which the packets arrive. A second field contains an *acknowledgement*: the number of the last frame that has been correctly received by the sending station. So no special acknowledgement frames are sent; acknowledgements are attached to data packets going the other way, a technique known as *piggybacking*.

Sometimes a third field is used to identify the *type* of the frame. This is done in more complex versions of the SWP (as described in section 4.4), where special frames are used for certain messages.

A frame can get lost or damaged during transmission. This means that it has to be resent. A 'resend action' can be triggered by the reception of a negative acknowledgement or by a timer, used to guard the time between the transmission of a frame and the reception of a (positive) acknowledgement from the other side. After a certain amount of time the timer produces a time-out, leading to the retransmission of one or more frames.

The possibility of retransmission of frames requires buffering of sent-but-not-yet-acknowledged frames. In the first SWP, specified in section 4.2, the buffer size is one. This means that after sending a frame the SWP process at station *A* has to wait until a frame with an acknowledgement from station *B* has arrived. In the more complex SWP's the buffer for sent-but-not-yet-acknowledged frames has a size greater than one. The outstanding frames form the *sending window*. With no outstanding frames the size of the sending window is zero. The maximum size of the sending window is related to the maximum buffer capacity.

Figure 4.1 shows three states of a sending window with maximum size 7 (frame numbers $0, \dots, 7$).

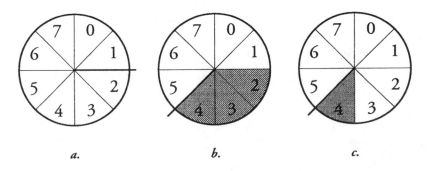

a.   b.   c.

Figure 4.1   Three states of a sending window with maximum size = 7
(*adapted from Tanenbaum89*)

In Figure 4.1.a the sending window is empty, no outstanding frames have to be acknowledged. The next frame to send is frame 2, as indicated with the thick line. In Figure 4.1.b the frames 2, 3 and 4 are sent, but not acknowledged. The next frame to send is frame 5. In Figure 4.1.c only frame 4 is sent, but not acknowledged. The frames 2 and 3 have been acknowledged.

The sending window is bounded by two pointers, *next-frame-to-acknowledge* and *next-frame-to-send*. The sending window is full when 'size' frames are buffered. Buffering of 'size+1' frames is not possible, because then the two pointers fall together and no distinction can be made between an empty window and a full window. When the sending window is full, the protocol is unable to accept data packets from a host, so this part of the communication between host and protocol will be blocked temporarily. The SWPs specified in section 4.3 and 4.4 use a sending window with a size greater than one.

It is also possible to buffer incoming data frames at the receiving part of the protocol. This means that the protocol can receive frames in a certain disorder, buffer them and send them in the right order to the receiving host when the missing frames have arrived. The incoming frames that can be buffered form the *receiving window*. The third SWP, specified in section 4.4, uses a receiving window with a size greater than one.

A communication protocol has to deal with channel errors and timing aspects. The reception of a damaged frame (usually noticed by the computation of a checksum) can be followed by the retransmission of one or more buffered frames or by the transmission of a special negative acknowledgement frame. It can also simply be ignored.

The loss of a frame cannot be detected by the receiving part of a protocol, this will lead to a time-out at the sending part. On the occurrence of a time-out one or all the outstanding frames can be retransmitted.

When there are no frames sent in one direction for a certain time the piggybacking of acknowledgements for received frames becomes a problem. This problem can be ignored or resolved by the transmission of a special acknowledgement frame.

Which options are applied in a certain protocol is partly determined by the basic structure of the protocol, partly it is a matter of free choice. For each protocol specified in the following sections, we will describe the applied options.

4.2 THE 'ONE BIT' PROTOCOL

4.2.1 GENERAL INTRODUCTION

The 'One Bit' protocol is the simplest Sliding Window Protocol: both the sending and receiving part of the protocol have a buffer of the size of one data packet, so the size of both the sending and receiving window is one.

In this simple protocol only data frames are sent. A data frame consists of a data packet and two additional numbers: the number of the frame itself and the number of the last correctly received frame. The sending part has to keep a transmitted data frame in its buffer until an acknowledgement is received. No new frames can be sent before this has occurred. This leads to an interleaving of sending and receiving. The sending part can only accept and transmit a new data packet from a host *after* the reception of an acknowledgement concerning the packet sent before. An acknowledgement has to be sent *before* the next frame can be received and acknowledged. This means that after the reception of a damaged frame (in case of a checksum error) or a frame with an unexpected acknowledgement, the old buffered data frame has to be retransmitted.

Frame numbers are restricted to 0 and 1. With these two numbers it is possible to make the distinction between two successive frames. These numbers can be implemented with one bit: the origin of the name of this protocol.

The maximum of 1 for the number of outstanding frames implies that only one timer is needed. This timer will produce a time-out when the acknowledgement for the outstanding frame does not arrive within a certain time.

Figures 4.2 to 4.4 show some examples of typical event sequences in the 'One Bit' protocol.

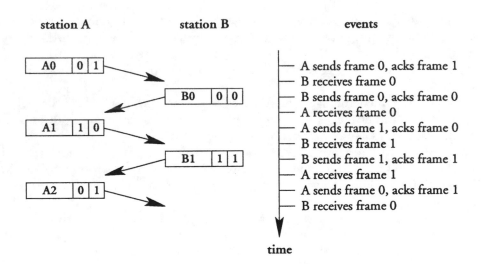

Figure 4.2   Normal interleaving of sending and receiving without errors or time-outs
(adapted from Tanenbaum89)

Figure 4.2 shows the normal operation of the 'One Bit' protocol. There are no transmission errors and no time-outs.

Figure 4.3 shows a frame from station *B* that gets lost. After the timer of station *A* times out, *A* sends its frame again to signal *B* that it has to retransmit the lost frame.

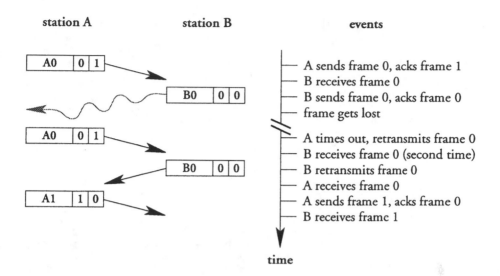

Figure 4.3   Recovery after the loss of a frame

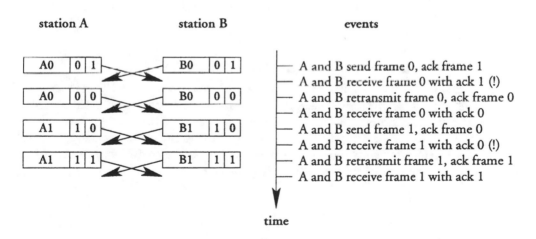

Figure 4.4   Permanent duplication caused by synchronous start

Figure 4.4 deserves special attention: every frame is sent twice, although no transmission errors occur. This inefficiency is caused by the synchronous start and subsequent synchronous operation of the two stations. Frames and acknowledgements cross each other over and over.

In the specification of the protocol we will assume a symmetrical general setting with two communicating stations, *A* and *B*. On each side we find the processes *IMP* (Interface Message Processor) and *TIMER*. The stations are connected by two channel processes for a full-duplex communication. The processes can communicate with each other by ports. The ports between IMPs and hosts are labelled with the characters *a*,

b, c and d. The ports between the processes mentioned above are labelled with the numbers $1, \ldots, 8$. See Figure 4.5.

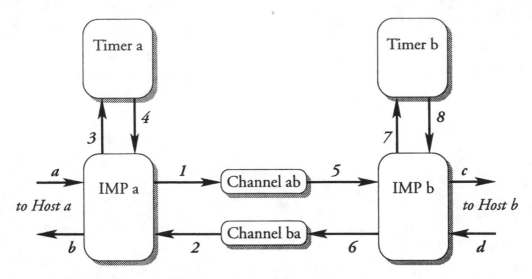

Figure 4.5   Processes and ports

4.2.2   SPECIFICATION OF THE 'ONE BIT' PROTOCOL

In the specification of the process modules we will give one general specification of the processes *IMP*, *TIM* and *CH*. The separate processes for the a- and b-sides will be created in the specification of the protocol in the process module *SWP1*. We will use a parameter to indicate the side. In the general specification of the processes we will use 'local' port names for communication ports. Later on they will be renamed to the real port names of Figure 4.5. Figure 4.6 shows the local port names.

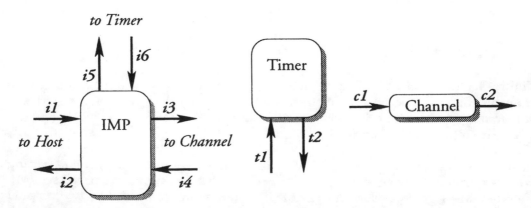

Figure 4.6   Local port names for separate processes

Before giving a specification of the various processes we will first specify the data concerned. In this simple protocol the data modules are simple too. We will use the data module *Bits* from the standard PSF library for the bits in a frame. The data module *Data* from the same library is used to model the data field in a frame.

4.2.2.1 Frames

In this protocol a frame consists of a data packet with two additional fields for frame numbers. The first number contains the number of the frame, the second number contains the number of the acknowledged frame. In the data module *Frames* the sort *FRAME* is specified. The function *frame* of this sort packs the three fields together. A channel can produce errors in a frame. Therefore, in the data module *Frames* the constant *ce* of the sort *FRAME* is specified.

```
data module Frames
begin

  exports
    begin
      sorts
        FRAME
      functions
        defr  :                      -> FRAME      -- default frame
        frame : DATA # BIT # BIT -> FRAME
        ce    :                      -> FRAME      -- checksum error
    end

  imports
    Bits,Data

end Frames
```

4.2.2.2 Sides

In the specification of the process modules we will use a parameter to indicate the *a*-side or *b*-side. Therefore a small data module *Sides* is introduced, which provides the sort *SIDE* and the constants *a-side* and *b-side*.

```
data module Sides
begin

  exports
    begin
      sorts
        SIDE
      functions
        a-side : -> SIDE
        b-side : -> SIDE
    end

end Sides
```

4.2.2.3 The Interface Message Processor

The process *IMP* is specified by a set of equations. Each equation has a well-defined role, which is explained in a comment line. State information (frame numbers, data packets) is transfered from one equation to another by arguments.

After the transmission of a frame the Interface Message Processor starts waiting for an incoming frame or a time-out. After the reception of a frame or a time-out a frame (new or old) is transmitted. Sending and receiving are interleaved. The initialization of this process requires special attention. When both sides start with waiting for a data packet to arrive from a host, a 'normal' communication sequence (cf. Figure 4.2) possibly will never emerge. On the other hand, when one side is initialized as a 'sender' and the other side as a 'receiver', the symmetry of the full-duplex protocol gets lost. In the specification given below the process *IMP* starts with waiting for a data packet to arrive from the host *or* a frame to arrive from the channel. When the expected frame (nr. 0) is received it is delivered to the host. The acknowledgement field of this frame is discarded, no sent frame is waiting for an acknowledgement. The reception of an unexpected frame (nr. 1) or a checksum error, normally leading to a retransmission of the frame last sent, is ignored. After an initial send action the process continues with waiting for an incoming frame. After an initial reception of an expected frame the process continues with waiting for a data packet to arrive from the host.

In the specification several abbreviations are used:

ftr = number of the frame to receive
fts = number of the frame to send
rac = received acknowledgement (number of the acknowledged frame)
rfr = number of the received frame

```
process module IMP
begin

   parameters
     TheSide
       begin
         sorts
           SD
         functions
           sd : -> SD
       end TheSide

   exports
     begin
       atoms
         ri1,si2 : DATA
         si3,ri4 : FRAME
         si5,ri6
       processes
         IMP : SD
     end

   imports
     Frames
```

```
processes
  READ       : SD # BIT # BIT
  SEND,REC   : SD # BIT # BIT # DATA
  DEL        : SD # BIT # BIT # BIT # BIT # DATA # DATA
  ACK        : SD # BIT # BIT # BIT # DATA

variables
  fts,ftr,rfr,rac : -> BIT
  dp1,dp2         : -> DATA

definitions
        -- Initialization, start with send or receive action:
  IMP(sd) =
        sum(dp1 in DATA,ri1(dp1).SEND(sd,bit0,bit0,dp1))
    +   sum(dp2 in DATA, sum(rac in BIT,ri4(frame(dp2,bit0,rac)).
            si2(dp2).READ(sd,bit0,bit1)))
    +   sum(dp3 in DATA, sum(rac in BIT,
            ri4(frame(dp3,bit1,rac)))).IMP(sd)
    +   ri4(ce).IMP(sd)

        -- Read data packet from host:
  READ(sd,fts,ftr) =
        sum(dp1 in DATA,ri1(dp1).SEND(sd,fts,ftr,dp1))

        -- Send frame to channel and start timer:
  SEND(sd,fts,ftr,dp1) =
        si3(frame(dp1,fts,invert(ftr))).si5.
            REC(sd,invert(fts),ftr,dp1)

        -- Receive frame from channel, checksum error or time-out:
  REC(sd,fts,ftr,dp1) =
        sum(dp2 in DATA, sum(rfr in BIT, sum(rac in BIT,
            ri4(frame(dp2,rfr,rac)).DEL(sd,fts,ftr,rfr,rac,dp1,dp2))))
    +   (ri4(ce) + ri6).SEND(sd,invert(fts),ftr,dp1)

        -- Deliver data packet to host if it is the expected one:
  DEL(sd,fts,ftr,rfr,rac,dp1,dp2) =
        [eq(ftr,rfr) = true] ->
            si2(dp2).ACK(sd,fts,invert(ftr),rac,dp1)
    +   [eq(ftr,rfr) = false] ->
            ACK(sd,fts,ftr,rac,dp1)

        -- Handle received acknowledgement:
  ACK(sd,fts,ftr,rac,dp1) =
        [eq(fts,invert(rac)) = true] ->
            READ(sd,fts,ftr)
    +   [eq(fts,invert(rac)) = false] ->
            SEND(sd,invert(fts),ftr,dp1)

end IMP
```

4.2.2.4 The Timer

The timer reads a (re-)start signal at port *t1* and sends a time-out signal at port *t2*.
No stop signal for the timer is needed. The specified process is very simple and does

not contain any specification of the process that leads to the moment that a time-out is generated. So after the timer is started, it can always generate a time-out. Sliding Window Protocols are resistant to premature time-outs.

```
process module TIM
begin

   parameters
     TheSide
        begin
          sorts
             SD
          functions
             sd : -> SD
        end TheSide

   exports
     begin
       atoms
          rt1,st2
       processes
          TIM : SD
     end

   processes
     TIM1 : SD

   definitions
     TIM(sd) = rt1.TIM1(sd)
     TIM1(sd) = st2.TIM(sd) + rt1.TIM1(sd)

end TIM
```

4.2.2.5 The Channel

The channel reads a frame, consisting of a data packet and two frame numbers (bits), at port $c1$. Three things can happen to the frame: it is delivered correctly at the other end of the channel (port $c2$), it is delivered at the same port with a checksum error or it is lost in the channel.

In this protocol it is possible that a station sends more than one frame into the channel before a frame has reached the other side of the channel. A station will, driven by time-outs or the reception of an unexpected acknowledgement, retransmit the last frame until an acknowledgement is received. We assume that the time interval after which the timer causes a time-out is chosen to be wide enough to permit a frame to reach the other side of the channel. In this protocol a maximum of two frames can be on their way in the channel. This maximum is reached in the event sequence shown in Figure 4.4.

Therefore we will specify the channel as a two data buffer with the possibility of destroying or losing data. The internal step *skip* indicates that the choice between correct and incorrect delivery of a frame is non-deterministic. When the outgoing port of the channel is blocked (no read actions are performed on port $c2$ to communicate with the channels send action on this port), a frame is lost. This is denoted by the atomic action *lost*. We will not assign a priority to the communication action over the *lost* action, so when the outgoing port is not blocked there is still a possibility of losing a frame.

The process module *CH* imports the data module *Frames* as introduced above.

```
process module CH
begin

   parameters
     TheSide
        begin
          sorts
            SD
          functions
            sd : -> SD
        end TheSide

   exports
     begin
       atoms
          rc1,sc2 : FRAME
          lost
       processes
          CH : SD
     end

   imports
     Frames

   processes
     CH1 : SD # FRAME
     CH2 : SD # FRAME # FRAME

   variables
     fr1,fr2 : -> FRAME

   definitions
     CH(sd) = sum(fr1 in FRAME,rc1(fr1).CH1(sd,fr1))

     CH1(sd,fr1) =
           sum(fr2 in FRAME,rc1(fr2).CH2(sd,fr1,fr2))
        +  skip.(sc2(fr1) + lost).CH(sd)
        +  skip.(sc2(ce) + lost).CH(sd)

     CH2(sd,fr1,fr2) =
           skip.(sc2(fr1) + lost).CH1(sd,fr2)
        +  skip.(sc2(ce) + lost).CH1(sd,fr2)

end CH
```

4.2.2.6 The 'One Bit' protocol

After the specification of the IMP's, timers and channels the complete SWP can be specified. We will call the merge of the six processes *SWP1*. In section 4.5 the communication between the SWP process and host processes is specified.

The process module *SWP1* imports the modules *IMP*, *TIM* and *CH* twice. In the first import the side-parameter is bound to the a-side and the local ports and the exported process are renamed to the ports and process corresponding to this side, in the second import the same is done for the b-side. So at this level the separate processes for the a- and b-side are created.

On the ports *1, ... , 8* a communication function is defined. Encapsulation is used to remove single send- and read-actions.

```
process module  SWP1
begin

   exports
      begin
         atoms
            c1,c2,c5,c6 : FRAME
            c3,c4,c7,c8
         processes
            SWP1
      end

   imports
      IMP {TheSide bound by [SD -> SIDE, sd -> a-side] to Sides
             renamed by [ri1 -> ra , si2 -> sb , si3 -> s1 , ri4 -> r2 ,
             si5 -> s3 , ri6 -> r4]},
      IMP {TheSide bound by [SD -> SIDE, sd -> b-side] to Sides
             renamed by [ri1 -> rd , si2 -> sc , si3 -> s6 , ri4 -> r5 ,
             si5 -> s7 , ri6 -> r8]},
      TIM {TheSide bound by [SD -> SIDE, sd -> a-side] to Sides
             renamed by [rt1 -> r3 , st2 -> s4]},
      TIM {TheSide bound by [SD -> SIDE, sd -> b-side] to Sides
             renamed by [rt1 -> r7 , st2 -> s8]},
      CH  {TheSide bound by [SD -> SIDE, sd -> a-side] to Sides
             renamed by [rc1 -> r1 , sc2 -> s5]},
      CH  {TheSide bound by [SD -> SIDE, sd -> b-side] to Sides
             renamed by [rc1 -> r6 , sc2 -> s2]}

   sets of atoms
      H =    {r1(f),s1(f),r2(f),s2(f),r5(f),s5(f),r6(f),s6(f) | f in FRAME}
           + {r3,s3,r4,s4,r7,s7,r8,s8}

   communications
      s1(f)|r1(f) = c1(f) for f in FRAME
      s2(f)|r2(f) = c2(f) for f in FRAME
      s5(f)|r5(f) = c5(f) for f in FRAME
      s6(f)|r6(f) = c6(f) for f in FRAME
      s3|r3 = c3
      s4|r4 = c4
      s7|r7 = c7
      s8|r8 = c8
```

```
definitions
  SWP1 = encaps(H,IMP(a-side) || TIM(a-side) || CH(a-side) ||
               IMP(b-side) || TIM(b-side) || CH(b-side))

end SWP1
```

This specification can be made concrete by importing it into a new process module and by binding the parameter of the module *Data*.

4.3   THE 'PIPELINING WITH GO BACK N' PROTOCOL

4.3.1   GENERAL INTRODUCTION

The 'Pipelining with Go Back N' protocol (in the sequel abbreviated to 'Pipelining' protocol) uses a sending window with a size greater than one. This means that a number of sent frames is buffered until an acknowledgement has been received from the other side. Strict interleaving of sending and receiving (as in the 'One Bit' protocol) is not necessary any more, a station can send a stream of frames to the other side without waiting for an acknowledgement. Only at the moment that the buffer of the sending window gets full does the need for an acknowledgement becomes urgent. As in the previous protocol only data frames are sent.

The sending part of the SWP buffers ('pipelines') outgoing frames. The maximum number of elements in the buffer determines the size of the sending window. If the sending window is full, no more data packets can be accepted from a host. In that case the data stream in one direction blocks.

Frame numbers are transmitted in a frame as n-bit numbers. Therefore the maximum size of a sending window is usually chosen to be $2^n - 1$, leading to frame numbers $0, \ldots, 2^n - 1$. The numbering of the frames is modulo n, n being the size of the sending window + 1. After frame number $2^n - 1$ frame number 0 is transmitted. The constant $2^n - 1$ will be called 'maxseq' in the sequel.

The receiving part of the SWP considers the acknowledgement of a frame with number f as an implicit acknowledgement of all the frames-sent-before-but-not-yet-acknowledged with a frame number less than f. So no separate acknowledgement for each sent frame is necessary: one incoming frame can acknowledge the correct transmission of 1, 2, 3, ... frames in the sending window. This means that, contrary to the 'One Bit' protocol of section 4.2, the data streams from A to B and B to A may differ significantly from each other in intensity, without one stream blocking the other.

The receiving window still has the size of one frame, so the data frames still have to arrive in the correct order. An out-of-order frame is thrown away, after having taken notice of the acknowledgement in it.

In this protocol the reception of a frame with a checksum error is simply ignored. The frame will time out at the other side and be retransmitted. On a time-out *all the frames in the sending window* are retransmitted. This is a consequence of the size of the receiving window: frames have to come in in order, so each frame received after a garbled frame or lost frame will be discarded anyhow. This strategy is called 'Go Back n'.

For each outstanding frame a timer is needed. This means that as many timers are needed as the size of the sending window. A 'timer queue' is an appropriate software data structure for the timers in this protocol. Such a queue will be used in the specification in this section.

The Figures 4.7 and 4.8 show some examples of typical event sequences in the 'Pipelining' protocol.

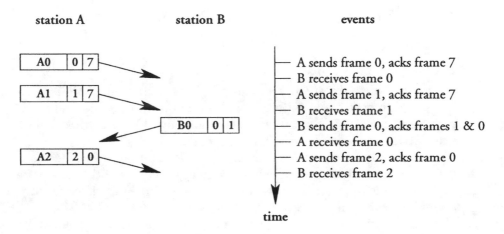

Figure 4.7   Normal event sequence without errors or time-outs

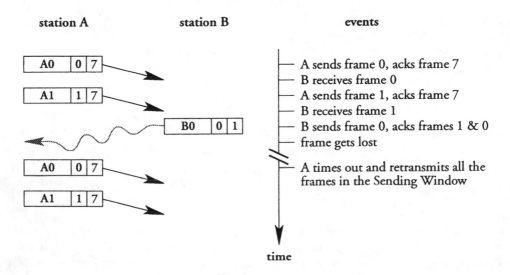

Figure 4.8   Recovery after loss of a frame

As in section 4.2 we will assume a symmetrical setting with two communicating sides, *A* and *B*. On each side we find the processes *IMP* and *TIMER*. The sending part of the IMP process now contains a buffer. The sides are connected by two channel processes. See Figure 4.9.

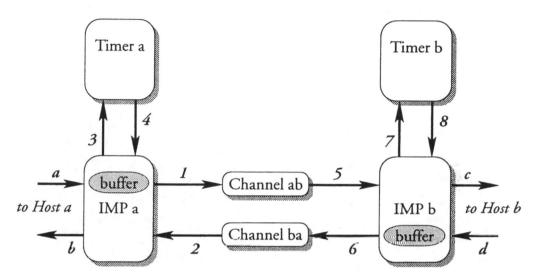

Figure 4.9   Processes and ports

4.3.2   SPECIFICATION OF THE 'PIPELINING' PROTOCOL

In the specifications several abbreviations are used. Most of them are the same as in section 4.2. The new ones are listed preceding the specification in which they are used for the first time.

In this protocol modulo arithmetic on frame numbers is used. To distinguish this arithmetic from 'normal' addition and subtraction special operators are introduced: +% and -% instead of + and - . These operators are defined as follows:

$x +\% \ y = (x + y) \ \textbf{mod} \ (maxseq + 1)$,

$x -\% \ y = (x + maxseq + 1 - y) \ \textbf{mod} \ (maxseq + 1)$.

'maxseq' stands for the highest frame number. The sending buffer has a size of 'maxseq' elements.

4.3.2.1   Frame Numbers

The operators +% and -% are specified in the data module *Frame-Numbers*. This module has a parameter *Bounds* with a constant *maxseq*. This constant can be bound to a natural number later on. The module imports the data module *Naturals* from the standard PSF library. With this import the standard module *Booleans* is imported too. The *mod* function from the module *Naturals* is used to implement the functions +% and -%.

```
data module Frame-Numbers
begin

  parameters
    Bounds
      begin
        functions
            maxseq : -> NATURAL
      end Bounds

  exports
    begin
      functions
        1    :                        -> NATURAL
        _+%_ : NATURAL # NATURAL -> NATURAL
        _-%_ : NATURAL # NATURAL -> NATURAL
      end

  imports
    Naturals

  variables
    x,y : -> NATURAL

  equations
    [1] 1 = s(zero)
    [2] x +% y = mod((x + y),(maxseq + s(zero)))
    [3] x -% y = mod((x - y),(maxseq + s(zero)))   when gte(x,y) = true
    [4] x -% y = (x + (maxseq + s(zero))) -% y     when lt(x,y) = true

end Frame-Numbers
```

4.3.2.2 Frames

As in the previous protocol a frame consists of a data packet with two additional fields for frame numbers. Frame numbers are now of the sort *NATURAL*. The imported standard module *Data* provides the sort *DATA* for the data field.

```
data module Frames
begin

  exports
    begin
     sorts
       FRAME
     functions
       defr  :                        -> FRAME      -- default frame
       frame : DATA # NATURAL # NATURAL -> FRAME
       ce    :                        -> FRAME      -- checksum error
     end

  imports
    Frame-Numbers,Data

end Frames
```

4.3.2.3 Windows

At certain moments in the protocol a test is required to verify whether a given frame number is in the sending window or not. In the data module *Windows* the function *in-Window* is specified, which performs this test. It should be noticed that the sending window contains the frames *low, ... ,upp*-1. Two local (hidden) functions (*seq* and *wrap*) take care of the fact that a window may consist of a row of successive natural numbers (such as {3,4,5}), but also may be 'wrapped' around zero (e.g. {6,7,0,1,2}).

```
data module  Windows
begin

  exports
    begin
      functions
        in-Window : NATURAL # NATURAL # NATURAL -> BOOLEAN
    end

  imports
    Frame-Numbers

  functions
    seq  : NATURAL # NATURAL # NATURAL -> BOOLEAN
    wrap : NATURAL # NATURAL # NATURAL -> BOOLEAN

  variables
    fr,low,upp : -> NATURAL

  equations
    [1]  in-Window(fr,low,upp) = or(seq(fr,low,upp),wrap(fr,low,upp))
    [2]  seq(fr,low,upp) = and(and(gt(upp,low),gte(fr,low)),lt(fr,upp))
    [3]  wrap(fr,low,upp) = and(lt(upp,low),or(gte(fr,low),lt(fr,upp)))

end Windows
```

4.3.2.4 Timers

Before we turn to the process modules two more small data modules are introduced. The data module *Timers* defines the signals *start* and *stop,* sent from the IMP to the timers as simple constants of the sort *TIMER-SIGNAL.* Only one constant of the sort *TIMER* is specified: again we will not specify timer details.

```
data module  Timers
begin

  exports
    begin
      sorts
        TIMER,TIMER-SIGNAL
      functions
        timer : -> TIMER
        start : -> TIMER-SIGNAL
        stop  : -> TIMER-SIGNAL
```

```
      end

  end Timers
```

4.3.2.5 Channel States

The channel specification in section 4.3.2.8 uses several 'channel states'. These states are specified as constants of the sort $CHANNEL\text{-}STATE$. The data module *ChannelStates* provides this sort and the channel states *accept, deliver, error* and *lost*.

```
    data module ChannelStates
    begin

      exports
        begin
          sorts
            CHANNEL-STATE
          functions
            accept  : -> CHANNEL-STATE
            deliver : -> CHANNEL-STATE
            error   : -> CHANNEL-STATE
            lost    : -> CHANNEL-STATE
        end

    end ChannelStates
```

4.3.2.6 The Interface Message Processor

As in section 4.2 we will give one general specification of the processes *IMP*, *TIM* and *CH*. In the general specification of these processes we will use the 'local' port names for communication ports as shown in Figure 4.6.

This protocol is not bound to a strict interleaving of sending and receiving of frames, as in the 'One Bit' protocol. A station can start by sending several frames before a frame is received, or vice versa. So in the specification of the IMP process we do not need a complex initialization expression.

In a sent frame the acknowledgement of the last received expected frame is represented by the frame number *ftr -% 1*.

A timer for each frame is started and stopped with a send action on port *i5*. It is not necessary to send a frame number to the timer process. This will be explained in the sequel.

In this protocol a sent frame is buffered in the sending window until an acknowledgement is received. We will import the standard PSF library module *Tables* to specify the buffers. In the import of this module the sort of the keys is bound to frame numbers, the sort of the items is bound to the sort *DATA* from the standard module *Data*. The sort *TABLE* is renamed to *BUFFER* in order to emphasize the meaning of the data type in this module.

As in the previous protocol read and send actions and the process *IMP* itself are exported by the module *IMP*.

Additional list of used abbreviations:

fta = number of the frame to be acknowledged (lower edge of the sending window)

tfs = number of the timed out frame to (re-)send.

```
process module IMP
begin

    parameters
      TheSide
        begin
          sorts
            SD
          functions
            sd : -> SD
        end TheSide

    exports
      begin
        atoms
          ri1,si2 : DATA
          si3,ri4 : FRAME
          si5     : TIMER-SIGNAL
          ri6
        processes
          IMP : SD
      end

    imports
      Frames,Timers,Windows,
      Tables {Keys bound by [KEY -> NATURAL, eq -> eq] to Frame-Numbers
              Items bound by [ITEM -> DATA, default-item -> default-data]
                  to Data renamed by
              [TABLE -> BUFFER, empty-table -> empty-buffer]}

    processes
      IMP   : SD # NATURAL # NATURAL # NATURAL # BUFFER
      SEND  : SD # NATURAL # NATURAL # NATURAL # DATA # BUFFER
      DEL   : SD # NATURAL # NATURAL # NATURAL # NATURAL # NATURAL # DATA #
              BUFFER
      ACK   : SD # NATURAL # NATURAL # NATURAL # NATURAL # BUFFER
      TIMO  : SD # NATURAL # NATURAL # NATURAL # NATURAL # BUFFER

    variables
      fts,fta,ftr,tfs,rfr,rac : -> NATURAL
      d,e                     : -> DATA
      buf                     : -> BUFFER

    definitions
            -- Initialization with empty buffer:
      IMP(sd) = IMP(sd,zero,zero,zero,empty-buffer)
```

```
                  -- Read data packet from host or receive frame or checksum
                  -- error from channel or time-out:
      IMP(sd,fts,fta,ftr,buf) =
              [eq((fts +% 1),fta) = false] ->
                   sum(d in DATA,ri1(d).SEND(sd,fts,fta,ftr,d,buf))
          +    sum(e in DATA,sum(rfr in NATURAL,sum(rac in NATURAL,
                   ri4(frame(e,rfr,rac)).DEL(sd,fts,fta,ftr,rfr,rac,e,buf))))
          +    ri4(ce).IMP(sd,fts,fta,ftr,buf)
          +    ri6.TIMO(sd,fts,fta,fta,ftr,buf)

                  -- Send frame to channel and start timer:
      SEND(sd,fts,fta,ftr,d,buf) =
              si3(frame(d,fts,ftr -% 1)).si5(start).
                   IMP(sd,fts +% 1,fta,ftr,insert(buf,d,fts))

                  -- Deliver received data packet to host if it is in the
                  -- expected frame:
      DEL(sd,fts,fta,ftr,rfr,rac,d,buf) =
              [eq(ftr,rfr) = true] ->
                   si2(d).ACK(sd,fts,fta,ftr +% 1,rac,buf)
          +    [eq(ftr,rfr) = false] ->
                   ACK(sd,fts,fta,ftr,rac,buf)

                  -- Handle acknowledged frames (stop timers and contract the
                  -- sending window):
      ACK(sd,fts,fta,ftr,rac,buf) =
              [in-Window(rac,fta,fts) = true] ->
                   si5(stop).ACK(sd,fts,fta +% 1,ftr,rac,buf)
          +    [in-Window(rac,fta,fts) = false] ->
                   IMP(sd,fts,fta,ftr,buf)

                  -- Handle time-out, retransmit all the frames in the sending
                  -- window:
      TIMO(sd,fts,tfs,fta,ftr,buf) =
              [in-Window(tfs,fta,fts) = true] ->
                   si3(frame(retrieve(buf,tfs),tfs,ftr -% 1)).si5(start).
                   TIMO(sd,fts,tfs +% 1,fta,ftr,buf)
          +    [in-Window(tfs,fta,fts) = false] ->
                   IMP(sd,fts,fta,ftr,buf)

  end IMP
```

4.3.2.7 The Timer

The Timer process is implemented using a queue of timers. For each sent frame a timer is appended to the queue. There is no need to use a timer table with keys representing frame numbers. A new timer, connected with the last frame sent, will be appended to the end of the queue. A time-out will only be generated by the timer at the front of the queue, that is connected to the longest outstanding frame. When a time-out occurs all the frames in the sending window are retransmitted. This means that the actual timer queue can be deleted and a new one built while retransmitting the buffered frames. A stop signal for a timer will only be given for the oldest frame in the sending window. This means that the timer that has been inserted first in the queue can be deleted.

As in the previous protocol, no specification is given of the mechanism that leads to the generation of a time-out.

The process module *TIM* imports the data module *Queues* from the standard PSF library to implement the timer queue. The sort of the queue elements, *Q-ELEMENT*, is bound to the sort *TIMER*, originating from the data module *Timers*. In the import of the data module *Queues* the sort *QUEUE* and the constant *empty-queue* are renamed to *TIMQ* and *etq*. This is done because the channel process uses a queue too (see the next section), and clashes of sorts and functions on a higher level have to be avoided.

```
process module TIM
begin

   parameters
     TheSide
       begin
         sorts
           SD
         functions
           sd : -> SD
       end TheSide

   exports
     begin
       atoms
         rt1 : TIMER-SIGNAL
         st2
       processes
         TIM : SD
     end

   imports
     Queues {Queue-parameter bound by [Q-ELEMENT -> TIMER,
             default-q-element -> timer] to Timers
             renamed by [QUEUE -> TIMQ, empty-queue -> etq]}

   processes
     TIM : SD # TIMQ

   variables
     tq : -> TIMQ

   definitions
         -- Initialization with an empty queue:
     TIM(sd) = TIM(sd,etq)

         -- Read start or stop signal, send time-out:
     TIM(sd,tq) =
         rt1(start).TIM(sd,enqueue(timer,tq))
     +   [eq(length(tq),zero) = false] ->
         (  rt1(stop).TIM(sd,dequeue(tq))
          + st2.TIM(sd,etq))

end TIM
```

4.3.2.8 The Channel

A station can send many frames into the channel before an acknowledgement has to be received from the other side. If the time-out interval for a frame has not been set too tightly, at most *maxseq* frames will be in the channel. However, we will abstract from this limitation and we will specify the channel behaviour by means of an *infinite queue*. Frames read at port *c1* are enqueued in the queue, frames delivered at port *c2* are dequeued.

In the specification below a *state parameter* determines what kind of action can be performed by the channel. A frame can be read at port *c1* in any state, so the "channel entrance" will never be blocked. In the state *accept*, if the queue is not empty, a non-deterministic choice is made concerning a transition to another state. In the state *deliver* a correct frame is delivered at port *c2* In the state *error* a frame with a checksum-error is delivered at the same port. In the state *lost* nothing is delivered; a frame is lost. This is specified by the non-communicating atomic action *lost*.

The process module *CH* uses a queue too. In the import of the module *Queues* the queue elements are bound to frames, the sort *QUEUE* and the constant *empty-queue* are renamed to *CHANNEL* and *empty-channel*. So no confusion will arise between this queue and the timer queue of the previous section.

```
process module CH
begin

   parameters
     TheSide
        begin
          sorts
            SD
          functions
            sd : -> SD
        end TheSide

   exports
     begin
       atoms
         rc1,sc2 : FRAME
         lost
       processes
         CH : SD
     end

   imports
     Queues{Queue-parameter bound by [Q-ELEMENT -> FRAME,
            default-q-element -> defr] to Frames
              renamed by [QUEUE -> CHANNEL, empty-queue -> empty-channel]},
     ChannelStates

   processes
     CH  : SD # CHANNEL # CHANNEL-STATE

   variables
     cq : -> CHANNEL
```

```
definitions
        -- Initialization with empty channel:
    CH(sd) = CH(sd,empty-channel,accept)

        -- Read a frame or make a non-deterministic choice between the
        -- three output-alternatives:
    CH(sd,cq,accept) =
            sum(fr in FRAME, rc1(fr).CH(sd,enqueue(fr,cq),accept))
        +   [eq(length(cq),zero) = false] ->
              ( skip.CH(sd,cq,deliver)
              + skip.CH(sd,cq,lost)
              + skip.CH(sd,cq,error))

        -- Read a frame or deliver a frame:
    CH(sd,cq,deliver) =
            sum(fr in FRAME, rc1(fr).CH(sd,enqueue(fr,cq),deliver))
        +   sc2(serve(cq)).CH(sd,dequeue(cq),accept)

        -- Read a frame or deliver a frame with a checksum error:
    CH(sd,cq,error) =
            sum(fr in FRAME, rc1(fr).CH(sd,enqueue(fr,cq),error))
        +   sc2(ce).CH(sd,dequeue(cq),accept)

        -- Read a frame or lose a frame:
    CH(sd,cq,lost) =
            sum(fr in FRAME, rc1(fr).CH(sd,enqueue(fr,cq),lost))
        +   lost.CH(sd,dequeue(cq),accept)

end CH
```

4.3.2.9 The 'Pipelining' protocol

The process module $SWP2$ is almost identical to the process module $SWP1$ of section 4.2.2.6. The timer signals *start* and *stop* in the communication between IMP and timer are new. This means that the atoms $r3$, $s3$, $r7$, $s7$ and $c3$, $c7$ now have an argument of the sort *TIMER-SIGNAL*. Another difference, of course, is the substitution of SWP2 for SWP1. As in the process module $SWP1$ the a-processes and b-processes are created by imports, parameter binding and renaming.

```
process module SWP2
begin

  exports
    begin
      atoms
        c1,c2,c5,c6 : FRAME
        c3,c7       : TIMER-SIGNAL
        c4,c8
      processes
        SWP2
    end
```

```
imports
    IMP {TheSide bound by [SD -> SIDE, sd -> a-side] to Sides
            renamed by [ri1 -> ra , si2 -> sb , si3 -> s1 , ri4 -> r2 ,
            si5 -> s3 , ri6 -> r4]},
    IMP {TheSide bound by [SD -> SIDE, sd -> b-side] to Sides
            renamed by [ri1 -> rd , si2 -> sc , si3 -> s6 , ri4 -> r5 ,
            si5 -> s7 , ri6 -> r8]},
    TIM {TheSide bound by [SD -> SIDE, sd -> a-side] to Sides
            renamed by [rt1 -> r3 , st2 -> s4]},
    TIM {TheSide bound by [SD -> SIDE, sd -> b-side] to Sides
            renamed by [rt1 -> r7 , st2 -> s8]},
    CH  {TheSide bound by [SD -> SIDE, sd -> a-side] to Sides
            renamed by [rc1 -> r1 , sc2 -> s5]},
    CH  {TheSide bound by [SD -> SIDE, sd -> b-side] to Sides
            renamed by [rc1 -> r6 , sc2 -> s2]}

sets of atoms
    H = {r1(f),s1(f),r2(f),s2(f),r5(f),s5(f),r6(f),s6(f) | f in FRAME}
        + {r3(t),s3(t),r7(t),s7(t) | t in TIMER-SIGNAL} + {r4,s4,r8,s8}

communications
    s1(f)|r1(f) = c1(f) for f in FRAME
    s2(f)|r2(f) = c2(f) for f in FRAME
    s5(f)|r5(f) = c5(f) for f in FRAME
    s6(f)|r6(f) = c6(f) for f in FRAME
    s3(t)|r3(t) = c3(t) for t in TIMER-SIGNAL
    s4|r4 = c4
    s7(t)|r7(t) = c7(t) for t in TIMER-SIGNAL
    s8|r8 = c8

definitions
    SWP2 = encaps(H,IMP(a-side) || TIM(a-side) || CH(a-side) ||
            IMP(b-side) || TIM(b-side) || CH(b-side))

end SWP2
```

This specification can be made concrete by importing it into a new process module and binding the parameters of the modules *Data* and *Frame-Numbers*.

4.4   THE 'NONSEQUENTIAL RECEIVE WITH SELECTIVE REPEAT' PROTOCOL

4.4.1   GENERAL INTRODUCTION

The last protocol of this chapter uses both a sending window and a receiving window with a size greater than one. The implications of a sending window with a size greater than one have been discussed in section 4.3.1. A receiving window with a size greater than one means that incoming frames are buffered until they can be sent to a host in the right order. So a nonsequential receiving of frames can be handled. This means that, contrary to the previous protocol, when a time-out occurs not all the frames in the sending window have to be retransmitted. In this protocol only the timed out frame is retransmitted. So the name of the protocol, 'Nonsequential Receive with Selective Repeat', should be clear now.

Special caution is required concerning the frame numbers and the size of the Sending and Receiving buffers. In certain cases an overlap of the sending window of station *A* and the receiving window of station *B* can cause problems.This happens if a sender retransmits a timed out frame that is in the receiving window of the receiver, the receiver possibly does not know if it is a new frame or a retransmission of an old one. In Figure 4.10a station *A* has transmitted the frames 0 .. 7, while no acknowledgements for these frames have been received so far. Station *B* has received all these frames except frame number 2, an acknowledgement for the frames 0 and 1 has been sent back. Now when station *B* receives a frame with the number 0 or 1 it is not clear if this is a new frame or a retransmission of an old frame with this number, due to a time-out caused by the loss of the acknowledgement of the previous reception of this frame. In Figure 4.10a the dark shaded area is the 'problem area'.

The solution to this problem is simple: both the sending window and the receiving window must be limited to a maximum size that is equal to half of the maximum frame number: *(maxseq + 1) div 2, maxseq* being an odd number. Now they can occupy only 'half of the circle', an ambiguous overlap is impossible. In Figure 4.10b station *A* has transmitted the frames *0, ... , 3*. No acknowledgements have been received. Station *B* has received all these frames except frame number 2, an acknowledgement for the frames 0 and 1 has been sent back. Now when station *B* receives a frame with the number 0 or 1 the frame is simply discarded because it is outside the receiving window.

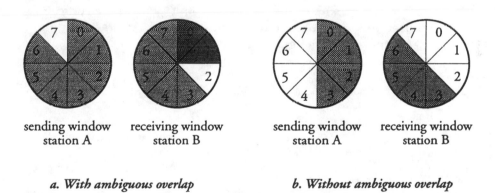

sending window　　　receiving window　　　　sending window　　　receiving window
station A　　　　　　station B　　　　　　　　station A　　　　　　station B

a. With ambiguous overlap　　　　　　　*b. Without ambiguous overlap*

Figure 4.10　The sending window and the receiving window in the 'Selective Repeat' Protocol

If the sending window is full, no more data packets can be received from a host and the data stream in one direction blocks. When the receiving window is full (all the frames in the window except the expected one have been received) the data stream between the hosts blocks too: all data packets from incoming frames are discarded until the expected frame is received.

As in the previous protocol an acknowledgement of frame number *n* is considered as an acknowledgement of all frames within the sending window with a number below *n*.

In this protocol not only data frames are transmitted, other types of frame are also used. These frames are used to get a minimal delay time caused by channel errors or a difference in traffic intensity in the two directions.

On the reception of a checksum error a frame with a negative acknowledgement, a *Nakframe*, is sent back. This frame does not contain a data field or a frame number, only the acknowledgement field is used to indicate which frame is expected. The reception of an out-of-order data frame also indicates an error, in this situation a Nakframe is sent back too. When a Nakframe is received the protocol responds with the retransmission of the expected frame: the oldest outstanding data frame (only if such a frame exists, of course). For reasons of efficiency not more than one Nakframe (request for retransmission) is sent for each expected frame.

Piggybacking of acknowledgements implies that, when no frames are sent in one direction (a host remains silent for a while), the sending window of the other side gets full and the protocol blocks because of a lack of acknowledgements. In the protocol of this section a separate timer is used to measure the time that has passed since the last unacknowledged frame has been received. The timer is started when an expected frame is received, it is stopped when a frame (with a piggybacked acknowledgement) is sent back. If this Acknowledgement Timer causes a time-out a special acknowledgement frame (an *Ackframe*) is sent to provide the other side with an acknowledgement of the frames received correctly so far. Like the Nakframe this frame does not contain a data field or a frame number. Only the acknowledgement field is used.

The use of three different frame types implies that in a frame a 'type field' is needed. So in this protocol the data frames contain four fields: type indicator, data packet, frame number and acknowledgement. The Nak- and Ackframes contain two fields: type indicator and acknowledgement.

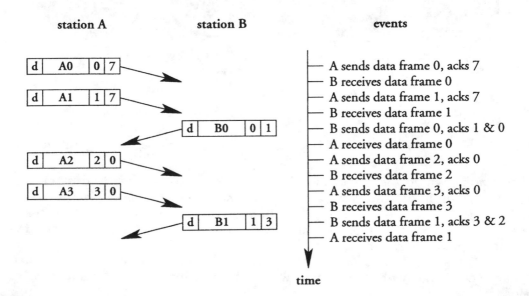

Figure 4.11   Normal event sequence, only data frames are transmitted

Figures 4.11 to 4.13 shows some examples of typical event sequences in the 'Nonsequential Receive' protocol. In the examples the frame numbers are restricted to $0, \ldots, 7$.

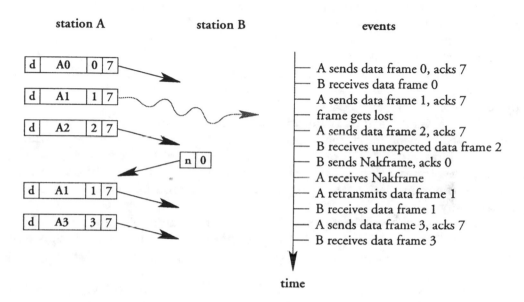

Figure 4.12 Error recovery with Nak frame and selective retransmission

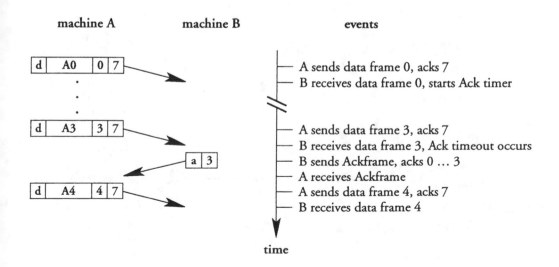

Figure 4.13 Separate acknowledgement with Ackframe

The use of Nakframes and Ackframes, as described above, does not guarantee a reliable data stream in one direction in the absence of a data stream in the other direction: after a particular sequence of events the protocol reaches a *livelock* state: although both the sender and the receiver can perform actions, no progress of the protocol is possible, as far as can be observed from the outside. Consider the state in which the sending window of a station A is full and the receiving window of a station B is empty. If, in this state, both the Nakframe and the Ackframe from B to A concerning the expected frame get lost, the protocol reaches a livelock state: A retransmits timed out frames to B but A will never receive any acknowledgement from B, because Nakframes and Ackframes are only sent once for a particular expected frame. As long as no data are sent from B to A, B remains silent.

There are several ways to avoid this livelock. If the Ack-timer is started on the reception of *every* incoming frame (expected or not), the loss of a particular Ackframe is not critical any more. If the restriction that a Nakframe is transmitted only once for a particular expected frame is dropped, every reception of an out-of-order frame will lead to the transmission of a Nakframe, so the loss of a particular Nakframe is not critical any more.

In this text we give a formal specification of the Sliding Window Protocols as presented in [Tan89]. This means that the specification will include this apparent livelock.

As with the previous protocols we give a diagram depicting the different processes. The IMP processes now contain two buffers, one for the sending part and one for the receiving part. The Acknowledgement Timer is situated within the TIMER process. See Figure 4.14.

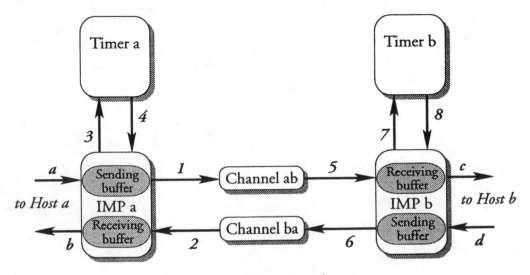

Figure 4.14   Processes and ports

4.4.2   SPECIFICATION OF THE 'NONSEQUENTIAL RECEIVE' PROTOCOL

For the arithmetic on frame numbers the modulo operators (-% , +%) are used, as defined in section 4.3.2.1. The size of the sending window and receiving window is equal to *(maxseq + 1) div 2, maxseq* being an odd number: $2^n - 1$. This is also the size of the sending and receiving buffers.

In this specification the standard PSF library modules *Booleans, Naturals, Data, Tables* and *Queues* are imported explicitly or implicitly. The data modules *Frame-Numbers, Sides, Windows* and *ChannelStates* and the process module *CH,* specified in previous sections, are used again.

4.4.2.1   Maximum Buffer Size

We start with a small data module Maxbuf-size. In this module a constant *maxbuf* of the sort *NATURAL* is specified, indicating the maximum buffer size. In this protocol the maximum buffer size is defined as *(maxseq + 1) div 2*. The constant *maxbuf* is used in the process module *IMP*.

```
data module  Maxbuf-size
begin

  exports
    begin
      functions
        maxbuf : -> NATURAL
    end

  imports
    Frame-Numbers

  equations
    [1] maxbuf = div(s(maxseq),s(s(zero)))

end Maxbuf-size
```

4.4.2.2   Frames

In this protocol three different frame types are used. So the data module *Frames* has to be rewritten. The three frame types *(data, ack, nak)* are specified as constants of the sort *FRAME-ID* (Frame Identifier). The constant *data* is abbreviated to *dat* because *data* is a reserved PSF keyword. For the equality test of two frame types the function *eq* is provided. Instead of using nine equations for specifying the equivalence of the frame types, the frame types are mapped on naturals with the local function *to-nat*. This makes it possible to use the function *eq*, as defined on naturals.

The different frame types are 'constructed' out of frame identifications, data packets and frame numbers with the functions *datafr* and *aknakfr*.

```
data module Frames
begin

  exports
    begin
      sorts
        FRAME-ID,FRAME
      functions
        dat     :                                         -> FRAME-ID
        ack     :                                         -> FRAME-ID
        nak     :                                         -> FRAME-ID
        eq      : FRAME-ID # FRAME-ID                      -> BOOLEAN
        defr    :                                         -> FRAME
        datafr  : FRAME-ID # DATA # NATURAL # NATURAL     -> FRAME
        aknakfr : FRAME-ID # NATURAL                       -> FRAME
        ce      :                                         -> FRAME
    end

  imports
    Frame-Numbers,Data

  functions
    to-nat : FRAME-ID -> NATURAL

  variables
    f1,f2 : -> FRAME-ID

  equations
    [1] to-nat(dat) = zero
    [2] to-nat(ack) = s(zero)
    [3] to-nat(nak) = s(s(zero))
    [4] eq(f1,f2) = eq(to-nat(f1),to-nat(f2))

end Frames
```

4.4.2.3 Timers

In this protocol the data module *Timers* provides an extra sort *ACK-TIMER* and a constant *ack-timer* for the Ack-Timer. The other sorts and functions are known from the module *Timers* used in the previous protocol.

```
data module Timers
begin

  exports
    begin
      sorts
        TIMER,TIMER-SIGNAL,ACK-TIMER
      functions
        timer : -> TIMER
        start : -> TIMER-SIGNAL
        stop  : -> TIMER-SIGNAL
        ack-timer   : -> ACK-TIMER
    end

end Timers
```

4.4.2.4   The Interface Message Processor

As in the specification of the previous protocols three parameterized process modules are specified for the processes *IMP*, *TIM* and *CH*. In the three process modules the names of the local ports are the same as in the previous SWP's. See Figure 4. 6.

The process expressions in the specification of the IMP process carry many arguments: frame numbers, separate buffers for sending and receiving, a boolean to indicate if a Nakframe has been sent. The abbreviations for the frame numbers are the same as in the previous specifications, the new ones are listed preceding the specification below.

The receiving window has a fixed size equal to the constant *maxbuf*. This means that a test can be performed whether a received frame is within the receiving window by the function *in-Window* with bounds *ftr* (frame to receive) and $ftr +\% maxbuf$. See the process expression *TORB* below.

The special acknowledgement timer (see section 4.4.1) is started after the reception of a data frame, it is explicitly stopped after the transmission of a Nakframe. The timer is implicitly stopped after the start of a timer for a transmitted data frame. See the specification of the timer process in section 4.4.2.5.

The process module *IMP* imports the standard PSF library module *Tables* for the Sending Buffer and the Receiving Buffer. The key is bound to frame numbers, the items are bound to *Data*. The name of the sort *TABLE* is renamed to *BUFFER*.

As in the previous protocols read and send actions and the process *IMP* itself are exported.

Additional list of abbreviations used:

  esb = empty sending buffer
  erb = empty receiving buffer
  sbuf = sending buffer
  rbuf = receiving buffer
  nfs = Nakframe sent

```
process module  IMP
begin

   parameters
      TheSide
        begin
          sorts
            SD
          functions
            sd : -> SD
        end TheSide

   exports
     begin
       atoms
          ri1,si2 : DATA
          si3,ri4 : FRAME
```

```
        si5      : TIMER-SIGNAL # NATURAL
        si5      : TIMER-SIGNAL # ACK-TIMER
        ri6      : NATURAL
        ri6      : ACK-TIMER
      processes
        IMP : SD
    end
```

imports
```
  Timers,Windows,Frames,Maxbuf-size,
  Tables {Keys bound by [KEY -> NATURAL, eq -> eq] to Frame-Numbers
          Items bound by [ITEM -> DATA, default-item -> default-data]
          to Data renamed by
          [TABLE -> BUFFER, empty-table -> empty-buffer]}
```

processes
```
  IMP     : SD # NATURAL # NATURAL # NATURAL # BUFFER # BUFFER # BOOLEAN
  SEND    : SD # NATURAL # NATURAL # NATURAL # DATA # BUFFER # BUFFER #
            BOOLEAN
  RECD    : SD # NATURAL # NATURAL # NATURAL # NATURAL # NATURAL #
            DATA # BUFFER # BUFFER # BOOLEAN
  DEL     : SD # NATURAL # NATURAL # NATURAL # NATURAL # BUFFER #
            BUFFER # BOOLEAN
  RECDNE  : SD # NATURAL # NATURAL # NATURAL # NATURAL # NATURAL #
            DATA # BUFFER # BUFFER # BOOLEAN
  TORB    : SD # NATURAL # NATURAL # NATURAL # NATURAL # NATURAL #
            DATA # BUFFER # BUFFER # BOOLEAN
  RECN    : SD # NATURAL # NATURAL # NATURAL # NATURAL # BUFFER #
            BUFFER # BOOLEAN
  ACK     : SD # NATURAL # NATURAL # NATURAL # NATURAL # BUFFER #
            BUFFER # BOOLEAN
  CHER    : SD # NATURAL # NATURAL # NATURAL # BUFFER # BUFFER # BOOLEAN
  TIMO    : SD # NATURAL # NATURAL # NATURAL # NATURAL # BUFFER #
            BUFFER # BOOLEAN
  ACKTO   : SD # NATURAL # NATURAL # NATURAL # BUFFER # BUFFER # BOOLEAN
```

variables
```
  fts,fta,ftr,tfs,rfr,rac : -> NATURAL
  d,e                     : -> DATA
  id                      : -> FRAME-ID
  sbuf,rbuf               : -> BUFFER
  nfs                     : -> BOOLEAN
```

definitions
```
        -- Initialization with two empty buffers, no Nakframe sent:
  IMP(sd) = IMP(sd,zero,zero,zero,empty-buffer,empty-buffer,false)

        -- Alternative composition of the possible events:
        -- read data from host if the sending buffer is not full:
  IMP(sd,fts,fta,ftr,sbuf,rbuf,nfs) =
        [eq((fts +% maxbuf),fta) = false] ->
            sum(d in DATA,ri1(d).SEND(sd,fts,fta,ftr,d,sbuf,rbuf,nfs))
```

```
                   -- or receive a data frame from the channel:
      +    sum(e in DATA, sum(rfr in NATURAL, sum(rac in NATURAL,
                ri4(datafr(dat,e,rfr,rac)).
                RECD(sd,fts,fta,ftr,rfr,rac,e,sbuf,rbuf,nfs))))
                   -- or receive a nak-frame from the channel:
      +    sum(rac in NATURAL, ri4(aknakfr(nak,rac)).
                RECN(sd,fts,fta,ftr,rac,sbuf,rbuf,nfs))
                   -- or receive an ack-frame from the channel:
      +    sum(rac in NATURAL, ri4(aknakfr(ack,rac)).
                ACK(sd,fts,fta,ftr,rac,sbuf,rbuf,nfs))
                   -- or receive a frame with a checksum error from the channel:
      +    ri4(ce).CHER(sd,fts,fta,ftr,sbuf,rbuf,nfs)
                   -- or receive a frame time-out from a timer:
      +    sum(tfs in NATURAL, ri6(tfs).
                TIMO(sd,fts,fta,ftr,tfs,sbuf,rbuf,nfs))
                   -- or receive an ack time-out from the ack-timer:
      +    ri6(ack-timer).ACKTO(sd,fts,fta,ftr,sbuf,rbuf,nfs)


                   -- Send data frame to the channel and start timer:
      SEND(sd,fts,fta,ftr,d,sbuf,rbuf,nfs) =
                si3(datafr(dat,d,fts,ftr -% 1)).si5(start,fts).
                IMP(sd,fts +% 1,fta,ftr,insert(sbuf,d,fts),rbuf,nfs)


                   -- Handle received data frame: expected or not?:
      RECD(sd,fts,fta,ftr,rfr,rac,e,sbuf,rbuf,nfs) =
                [eq(ftr,rfr) = true] ->
                   DEL(sd,fts,fta,ftr,rac,sbuf,insert(rbuf,e,rfr),nfs)
      +    [eq(ftr,rfr) = false] ->
                   RECDNE(sd,fts,fta,ftr,rfr,rac,e,sbuf,rbuf,nfs)


                   -- Deliver received data packet to host, start ack-timer:
      DEL(sd,fts,fta,ftr,rac,sbuf,rbuf,nfs) =
                [in-table(rbuf,ftr) = true] ->
                   si2(retrieve(rbuf,ftr)).
                   DEL(sd,fts,fta,ftr +% 1,rac,sbuf,delete(rbuf,ftr),false)
      +    [in-table(rbuf,ftr) = false] ->
                   si5(start,ack-timer).ACK(sd,fts,fta,ftr,rac,sbuf,rbuf,nfs)


                   -- Handle unexpected received data frame: Nakframe sent?:
      RECDNE(sd,fts,fta,ftr,rfr,rac,e,sbuf,rbuf,nfs) =
                [nfs = false] ->
                   si3(aknakfr(nak,ftr -% 1)).si5(stop,ack-timer).
                   TORB(sd,fts,fta,ftr,rfr,rac,e,sbuf,rbuf,true)
      +    [nfs = true] ->
                   TORB(sd,fts,fta,ftr,rfr,rac,e,sbuf,rbuf,nfs)


                   -- Handle unexpected data frame: place it in in receiving
                   -- buffer if it is in the receiving window and it has not been
                   -- received before
      TORB(sd,fts,fta,ftr,rfr,rac,e,sbuf,rbuf,nfs) =
                [and(in-Window(rfr,ftr,ftr +% maxbuf),
                 not(in-table(rbuf,rfr))) = true] ->
                   ACK(sd,fts,fta,ftr,rac,sbuf,insert(rbuf,e,rfr),nfs)
      +    [and(in-Window(rfr,ftr,ftr +% maxbuf),
                 not(in-table(rbuf,rfr))) = false] ->
                   ACK(sd,fts,fta,ftr,rac,sbuf,rbuf,nfs)
```

```
            -- Handle received Nakframe: retransmit oldest outstanding
            -- frame if it is in the sending window:
RECN(sd,fts,fta,ftr,rac,sbuf,rbuf,nfs) =
        [in-Window(rac +% 1,fta,fts) = true] ->
            si3(datafr(dat,retrieve(sbuf,rac +% 1),rac +% 1,ftr -% 1)).
            si5(start,rac +% 1).ACK(sd,fts,fta,ftr,rac,sbuf,rbuf,nfs)
    +   [in-Window(rac +% 1,fta,fts) = false] ->
            ACK(sd,fts,fta,ftr,rac,sbuf,rbuf,nfs)


            -- Handle acknowledged frames: stop timer, remove frames from
            -- sending window :
ACK(sd,fts,fta,ftr,rac,sbuf,rbuf,nfs) =
        [in-Window(rac,fta,fts) = true] ->
            si5(stop,fta).ACK(sd,fts,fta +% 1,ftr,rac,sbuf,rbuf,nfs)
    +   [in-Window(rac,fta,fts) = false] ->
            IMP(sd,fts,fta,ftr,sbuf,rbuf,nfs)


            -- Handle checksum error: send nakframe (if not sent before):
CHER(sd,fts,fta,ftr,sbuf,rbuf,nfs) =
        [nfs = false] ->
            si3(aknakfr(nak,ftr -% 1)).si5(stop,ack-timer).
            IMP(sd,fts,fta,ftr,sbuf,rbuf,true)
    +   [nfs = true] ->
            IMP(sd,fts,fta,ftr,sbuf,rbuf,true)


            -- Handle time-out for a single frame:
TIMO(sd,fts,fta,ftr,tfs,sbuf,rbuf,nfs) =
        si3(datafr(dat,retrieve(sbuf,tfs),tfs,ftr -% 1)).
            si5(start,tfs).IMP(sd,fts,fta,ftr,sbuf,rbuf,nfs)


            -- Handle ack-time-out:
ACKTO(sd,fts,fta,ftr,sbuf,rbuf,nfs) =
        si3(aknakfr(ack,ftr -% 1)).IMP(sd,fts,fta,ftr,sbuf,rbuf,nfs)


    end IMP
```

4.4.2.5 The Timer

In this protocol the timer process cannot be implemented with a queue, as in the previous protocol. The retransmission of a single frame (caused by a time-out or the reception of a Nakframe, checksum error) disturbs the correspondence between the sending window and a 'timer queue', see Figure 4.15.

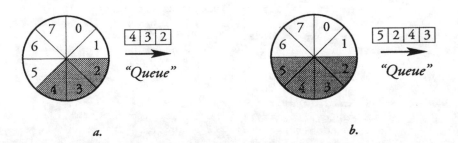

Figure 4.15. Sending window and 'timer queue'.

In Figure 4.15a the frames 2, 3 and 4 are transmitted. The 'timer queue' contains the frame numbers. Figure 4.15b shows the sending window and the 'timer queue' after a time-out of the timer for frame 2, the retransmission of this frame and the transmission of frame 5. Now frame number 3 is the 'oldest' frame, so that frame will eventually cause a time-out, followed by its retransmission. In this case the 'lowest' frame in the sending window is not retransmitted. This makes it necessary to remember the frame number with the timer and, on a time-out, to send the frame number to the IMP process.

When in the state of Figure 4.15.b an acknowledgement of the frames 2 and 3 has been received, the timers for these frames have to be removed from the 'queue'. It is clear that for frame number 2 this is not a simple dequeueing action. So in this protocol we will not use a queue but a *table* of timers. A timer can be inserted in the table (with the corresponding frame number as the key value) and deleted from the table.

As mentioned above an ack-timer is used to take care of the transmission of acknowledgements if one side of the protocol stays idle for a long time. This timer is started at the moment an expected data frame has been received. The ack-timer is stopped after a data frame or a Nakframe has been transmitted. These events do not guarantee that the ack-timer has been started before, so the timer can be stopped without having been started. The transmission of a data frame is followed by the start of a timer for that frame. In the specification below this start-command is used to stop the ack-timer. After the transmission of a Nakframe an explicit stop-command is received from the IMP process.

In the specification below the status of the ack-timer is represented by a boolean argument *atr* (ack-timer running).

The abbreviation 'ett' stands for 'empty timer table', 'ttab' stands for 'timer table'. A particular timer *fn* is running if the condition *in-table(ttab,fn)* is true.

The process module *TIM* uses the data module *Tables* to implement the 'Timer Table'. The keys are bound to frame numbers, the items are bound to timers. The name of the sort *TABLE* is renamed to *TTAB*.

```
process module TIM
begin

   parameters
     TheSide
       begin
         sorts
           SD
         functions
           sd : -> SD
       end TheSide

   exports
     begin
       atoms
         rt1 : TIMER-SIGNAL # NATURAL
         rt1 : TIMER-SIGNAL # ACK-TIMER
         st2 : NATURAL
         st2 : ACK-TIMER
```

```
            processes
                TIM : SD
            end

        imports
            Frames,
            Tables {Keys bound by [KEY -> NATURAL, eq -> eq] to Frame-Numbers
                    Items bound by [ITEM -> TIMER, default-item  -> timer]
                        to Timers renamed by [TABLE -> TTAB, empty-table -> ett]}

        processes
            TIM  : SD # TTAB # BOOLEAN
            TIM1 : SD # BOOLEAN # NATURAL # TTAB # BOOLEAN
            TIM2 : SD # TTAB # BOOLEAN

        variables
            ttab   : -> TTAB
            atr    : -> BOOLEAN

        definitions
                -- Initialization with empty timer table, no Ack-timer started:
            TIM(SD) = TIM(sd,ett,false)

                -- Read different signals for the timer queue, Ack-timer or
                -- send time-out:
            TIM(sd,ttab,atr) =
                sum(fn1 in NATURAL, rt1(start,fn1)
                    TIM(sd,insert(ttab,timer,fn1),false))
            + rt1(start,ack-timer).TIM(sd,ttab,true)
            + rt1(stop,ack-timer).TIM(sd,ttab,false)
            + sum(fn2 in NATURAL,
                [in-table(ttab,fn2) = true] ->
                    (rt1(stop,fn2) + st2(fn2)).TIM(sd,delete(ttab,fn2),atr))
            + [atr = true] -> st2(ack-timer).TIM(sd,ttab,false)

        end TIM
```

4.4.2.6 The Channel

Although the contents of the frames have changed, the process module *CH* is exactly the same as in section 4.3.2.8: an infinite queue of frames. We do not show this module here. (Note: the change of frame contents is specified in the data module *Frames*.)

4.4.2.7 The 'Nonsequential Receive' Protocol

The process module *SWP3* differs from the process modules *SWP1* and *SWP2* in several predictable details: the substitution of *SWP3* for *SWP1/2* and the expansion of the communication between the processes *IMP* and *TIMER* with frame numbers and an ack-timer, leading to a new definition of the atoms, sets of atoms and communications concerning the read-actions and send-actions between the processes *IMP* and *TIMER*.

```
process module SWP3
begin

  exports
    begin
      atoms
        c1,c2,c5,c6 : FRAME
        c3,c7       : TIMER-SIGNAL # NATURAL
        c3,c7       : TIMER-SIGNAL # ACK-TIMER
        c4,c8       : NATURAL
        c4,c8       : ACK-TIMER
      processes
        SWP3
    end

  imports
    IMP {TheSide bound by [SD -> SIDE, sd -> a-side] to Sides
           renamed by [ri1 -> ra , si2 -> sb , si3 -> s1 , ri4 -> r2 ,
           si5 -> s3 , ri6 -> r4]},
    IMP {TheSide bound by [SD -> SIDE, sd -> b-side] to Sides
           renamed by [ri1 -> rd , si2 -> sc , si3 -> s6 , ri4 -> r5 ,
           si5 -> s7 , ri6 -> r8]},
    TIM {TheSide bound by [SD -> SIDE, sd -> a-side] to Sides
           renamed by [rt1 -> r3 , st2 -> s4]},
    TIM {TheSide bound by [SD -> SIDE, sd -> b-side] to Sides
           renamed by [rt1 -> r7 , st2 -> s8]},
    CH  {TheSide bound by [SD -> SIDE, sd -> a-side] to Sides
           renamed by [rc1 -> r1 , sc2 -> s5]},
    CH  {TheSide bound by [SD -> SIDE, sd -> b-side] to Sides
           renamed by [rc1 -> r6 , sc2 -> s2]}

  sets of atoms
    H =   {r1(f),s1(f),r2(f),s2(f),r5(f),s5(f),r6(f),s6(f) | f in FRAME}
        + {r3(t,f),s3(t,f),r7(t,f),s7(t,f) | t in TIMER-SIGNAL,
            f in NATURAL}
        + {r3(t,a),s3(t,a),r7(t,a),s7(t,a) | t in TIMER-SIGNAL,
            a in ACK-TIMER}
        + {r4(f),s4(f),r8(f),s8(f) | f in NATURAL}
        + {r4(a),s4(a),r8(a),s8(a) | a in ACK-TIMER}

  communications
    s1(f)|r1(f) = c1(f) for f in FRAME
    s2(f)|r2(f) = c2(f) for f in FRAME
    s5(f)|r5(f) = c5(f) for f in FRAME
    s6(f)|r6(f) = c6(f) for f in FRAME
    s3(t,f)|r3(t,f) = c3(t,f) for t in TIMER-SIGNAL, f in NATURAL
    s3(t,a)|r3(t,a) = c3(t,a) for t in TIMER-SIGNAL, a in ACK-TIMER
    s4(f)|r4(f) = c4(f) for f in NATURAL
    s4(a)|r4(a) = c4(a) for a in ACK-TIMER
    s7(t,f)|r7(t,f) = c7(t,f) for t in TIMER-SIGNAL, f in NATURAL
    s7(t,a)|r7(t,a) = c7(t,a) for t in TIMER-SIGNAL, a in ACK-TIMER
    s8(f)|r8(f) = c8(f) for f in NATURAL
    s8(a)|r8(a) = c8(a) for a in ACK-TIMER
```

```
definitions
    SWP3 = encaps(H,IMP(a-side) || TIM(a-side) || CH(a-side) ||
            IMP(b-side) || TIM(b-side) || CH(b-side))

end SWP3
```

This specification can be made concrete by importing it into a new process module and binding the parameters of the modules *Data* and *Frame-Numbers*.

4.5 THE EXTERNAL BEHAVIOUR OF AN SWP

In this section we will specify the communication between the Network Layer Level of two stations (the 'hosts') and a Sliding Window Protocol. We have postponed the discussion of this subject until the specification of the three SWP's was completed in order to emphasize the transparency of a communication protocol (the transfer of data packets from host to host should be independent of the protocol that is used). And, on the other hand, to discuss the impact of the differences between the three protocols on their external performance.

4.5.1 THE COMMUNICATION BETWEEN SWP AND HOSTS

We suppose a general setting in which the hosts communicate with a SWP by means of two ports, one for sending data packets, one for receiving data packets (*a,b* and *c,d* in Figure 4.16).

Figure 4.16 Ports between SWP and Hosts

The processes *HOSTa* and *HOSTb* are sending and receiving a continuous stream of data packets. As discussed above, the data packets are sent and have to be received in order.

In the specification of the processes *HOSTa* and *HOSTb* we will define only one process module *Host*. By import, parameter binding and renamings we will create the separate processes *HOSTa* and *HOSTb*.

The process module *Host* uses two 'local' ports, *h1* and *h2*, at which a data packet is sent or read. These ports will be renamed to the actual ports *a, b, c, d*. The data module *Data* is imported for the sort *DATA* of the data packets.

```
process module Host
begin

  parameters
    TheSide
      begin
        sorts
          SD
        functions
          sd : -> SD
      end TheSide

  exports
    begin
      atoms
        sh1,rh2 : DATA
      processes
        HOST : SD
    end

  imports
    Data

  definitions
    HOST(sd) = (sum(d in DATA,sh1(d)) + sum(e in DATA,rh2(e))).HOST(sd)

end Host
```

In the process module *Communication* everything finally comes together: two *HOST* processes and the *SWP* process are imported, merged and encapsulated. The ports of the hosts are renamed to actual ports *a, b, c, d* cf. Figure 4.16.

In this module the protocol is called SWP. By adding a number 1, 2 or 3 the module can be used in combination with one of the three Sliding Window Protocols, specified in the previous sections.

```
process module Communication
begin

  exports
    begin
      atoms
        ca,cb,cc,cd : DATA
      processes
        COMM
    end

  imports
    Host {TheSide bound by [SD -> SIDE, sd -> a-side] to Sides
          renamed by [sh1 -> sa, rh2 -> rb]},
    SWP,
    Host {TheSide bound by [SD -> SIDE, sd -> b-side] to Sides
          renamed by [sh1 -> sd, rh2 -> rc]}

  sets of atoms
    H = {sa(d),ra(d),sb(d),rb(d),sc(d),rc(d),sd(d),rd(d) | d in DATA}
```

```
communications
   sa(d)|ra(d)  = ca(d)  for d in DATA
   sb(d)|rb(d)  = cb(d)  for d in DATA
   sc(d)|rc(d)  = cc(d)  for d in DATA
   sd(d)|rd(d)  = cd(d)  for d in DATA

definitions
   COMM = encaps(H, HOST(a-side) || SWP || HOST(b-side) )

end Communication
```

The specification of the host processes in this section is based on the independence of the sending and the receiving of data packets: after a data packet has been sent or received another send action or a receive action is possible. This means for example that this specification can lead to a sequence of n send actions, $n = 1 .. k$, without a receive action.

From the description of the protocols in the previous sections it may be clear that not all the protocols can process a continuous sequence of send actions.

The 'One Bit' protocol of section 4.2 requires strict interleaving of sending and receiving. The actual behaviour of a host, using this protocol for data transfer, will be restricted to the following expression:

```
HOST(sd) =(sum(d in DATA, sh1(d)).sum(e in DATA, rh2(e))).HOST(sd)
```

The 'Pipelining' protocol and the 'Nonsequential Receive' protocol do not have such a restriction. The 'Pipelining' protocol of section 4.3 will block when the sending buffer is full. From that moment on no more data packets can be read from a host. So for this protocol the specification of a host process should be something like

```
HOST(sd) = [host-enabled = true] -> sum(d in DATA, sh1(d)).HOST(sd)
           + sum(e in DATA, rh2(e)).HOST(sd)
```

The boolean condition *host-enabled* corresponds to the condition 'eq(fts + %1,fta) = false' (the sending buffer is not full), introduced in the IMP process in section 4.3.2.6. If this condition is false (the sending buffer is full), the specified IMP process is unable to perform a read action on port a, so no communication can take place with the host on this port. This 'implicit' blockade of communication makes an explicit blockade of a send action of the host by means of the boolean condition 'host enabled' superfluous. So for this protocol the specification of the Host process, given in the beginning of this section, can be used.

The 'Nonsequential Receive' protocol of section 4.4 is the only protocol of the three that can process a continuous stream of data packets in one direction without any data transfer in the other direction, thus establishing a 'simplex' connection between two hosts. This option is made possible by the introduction of a special Ackframe: a receiving host can send an acknowledgement without sending a data frame. So for this protocol the specification of the host process, given in the beginning of this section, will do too.

4.5.2   THE PERFORMANCE OF THE THREE PROTOCOLS

Comparing the three protocols, we can conclude that the 'Nonsequential Receive' protocol is the most flexible one: it even permits a simplex communication between two hosts. The 'One Bit' protocol is extremely inflexible: only when two hosts send data packets to each other at the same rate will this protocol work. The 'Pipelining' protocol can handle differences in traffic density up to a certain degree: when the sending buffer gets full this protocol will block.

Apart from the handling of a difference in traffic density between the Hosts, the performance of a protocol also depends on the 'error rate' of the channels. If a channel with a high error rate is used, the 'Pipelining' protocol becomes even more inefficient: the reception of a bad frame with a checksum error is ignored, leading to a time-out whereafter *all* the frames in the sending window are retransmitted. If this happens many times, the performance of the protocol will decrease significantly.

4.6   SUMMARY

Sliding Window Protocols are used for reliable data transmission over faulty channels in two directions. A Sliding Window Protocol buffers sent-but-not-yet-acknowledged frames in the sending window. Received-but-not-yet-expected frames may be buffered in the receiving window. No separate acknowledgement messages are sent: acknowledgements are piggybacked to dataframes.

In this chapter three Sliding Window Protocols, taken from the literature, are specified in PSF. The three protocols differ in the size of the sending window and the receiving window and in the way errors and differences in traffic density are handled.

The simplest protocol, the 'One Bit' protocol, has a sending window and a receiving window with the size of one element. This small window size introduces some initialization problems, possibly leading to many frame retransmissions.

The 'Pipelining with Go Back n' protocol has a sending window with a size of more than one element. The receiving window still has a size of one element. The enlargement of the sending window leads to a more flexible protocol. However, frequent channel errors may lead to many retransmissions and a decrease of the performance of the protocol.

In the 'Nonsequential Receive with Selective Retransmision' protocol both the sending window and the receiving window have a size of more than one element. This makes the protocol the most flexible one of the three in handling differences in traffic density. For efficiency reasons special purpose frames (Ackframes and Nakframes) are used. This may lead to a livelock, as described in section 4.4.

The increasing complexity of the protocols is reflected in the PSF specifications. In the 'One Bit' protocol both data modules and process modules are simple. In the 'Pipelining' protocol and the 'Nonsequential Receive' protocol more complex data types such as queues and tables are used to model channels and buffers. The process modules cannot be qualified as simple any more.

In the specification of the protocol processes the 'a-side' and 'b-side' processes are not specified separately, but they are created by a double import of a single generic process, the binding of a 'side-parameter' and renamings on communication ports.

4.7 BIBLIOGRAPHICAL NOTES

The three Sliding Window Protocols of this chapter were taken from *Computer Networks* by A.S. Tanenbaum ([Tan89]).

This is not the first text on Sliding Window Protocols in the context of formal specification. In [Vaa86] and [Wam92b] a specification in the formalism ACP and the correctness proof of two different versions of the 'One Bit' protocol is given. In [Mid86] the 'Pipelining' protocol is specified in ACP. In [Gro87] this protocol is specified and verified. In [Bru91a] all three protocols are specified in both ACP and PSF. This text has been used as the basis for this chapter.

The livelock in the third Sliding Window Protocol was discovered by Jan Friso Groote. A short reference to it can be found in the Propositions, added to his Ph.D. Thesis ([Gro91]).

Chapter 5
The Amoeba Transaction Protocol

J.J. Brunekreef

5.1 Introduction

The Amoeba Distributed Operating System uses a *Transaction Protocol* for the communication between different processes running under the supervision of the Operating System. A transaction is a basic form of information exchange between two processes, consisting of a *request* followed by a *reply*. Contrary to a Connection Oriented Protocol a Transaction Protocol does not establish a permanent (logical) connection between two communicating processes. For each transaction a connection is built up. As soon as the transaction is finished the connection is broken. The choice of a Transaction Protocol in favour of a Connection Oriented Protocol is based on the observation that in a distributed operating system most communications within a network do not imply massive data transport during a long time. As a result the overhead costs of building up and maintaining a permanent connection between two processes will be (too) high.

In the Amoeba Operating System transactions take place between a *Client* process and a *Server* process. A Client process sends a request to the network. This request can be answered by a Server process with a reply. In order to increase the performance and the fault tolerance of the operating system several Server processes may provide the same service. When a specific Server crashes or is temporarily busy another one can take over its task.

As in all communication protocols, acknowledgements are needed for reliable communications. In the Amoeba Transaction Protocol, abbreviated to ATP in the sequel, an *acknowledgement message* from Client to Server is used to report the reception of a reply. The reply itself serves as an acknowledgement of the reception of a request. The acknowledgement message may be replaced by a next request from the same Client to the same Server in a consecutive transaction. Besides requests, replies and acknowledgements the ATP uses *enquiry messages, signal messages* and several timers. The use of these messages and timers will be explained in section 5.2, in which a more detailed description of the ATP is given. In sections 5.3 and 5.4 a specification of the ATP is given.

5.2   A GENERAL DESCRIPTION OF THE AMOEBA TRANSACTION PROTOCOL

The inter-process communication in the Amoeba Distributed Operating System does not fit into the ISO/OSI reference model. Three layers are distinguished:
- the *Physical Layer* provides a physical connection.
- the *Port Layer* provides a 'datagram' service from one port to another. A message is delivered to the right spot at most once. In this layer a lot of attention is paid to security aspects. Messages between processes use an 'encoded' source address and destination address. We will not go into the details of this protection mechanism. The Port Layer does not deal with reliability aspects such as acknowledgements, time-outs and retransmissions. These aspects are part of the Transaction Layer Level.
- the *Transaction Layer* provides a reliable 'transaction' service between processes. This layer will be described in detail in section 5.2.1.

In the ATP a message consists of a header, which may be followed by a data part. The header has a length of 40 bytes. The size of the data part can vary from 0 to 32 kilobytes. The first 20 bytes of the header are used by the Port Layer: 2 bytes for the length of the data part and 3*6 bytes for the destination address, the reply address and extra protection information. The other 20 bytes of the header may be used by higher levels. Control messages and Signal messages (see section 5.2.1) only consist of a header.

In the OSI model security and routing aspects are dealt with in the higher layers, controlled by user-defined protocols. In the Amoeba Distributed Operating System these communication aspects are part of a lower layer, which is controlled by the operating system.

5.2.1   THE TRANSACTION LAYER

At this level a process may act as a *Client*, asking for a service, or as a *Server*, providing a specific service to other processes in the network. A *transaction* between Client and Server basically consists of a Client's request to a Server and a reply from the Server to the Client. A transaction starts with a *transaction call*, issued by a Client. For a Client a transaction call blocks: that is during a transaction the Client cannot perform other actions. However, after being interrupted by some other process, the Client can decide to cancel the transaction by sending a *signal message* to the Server.

At the start of a transaction a *transaction record* is created, both by the Client process and by the Server process. This record contains information about the connection between the processes and a sequence number for consecutive transactions between the two processes. When a transaction is finished the Client transaction record is deleted, unless it is followed by another transaction between the same

Client and Server within a certain time. The Server transaction record is always deleted.

The Transaction Protocol has to provide a reliable communication between a Client and a Server. A Server process may crash, messages can get lost or be damaged. Therefore besides data messages, control messages and timers are used. The ATP uses two types of control messages: *acknowledgements* and *enquiries*. A control message consists of a header only; no data part is involved.

Three different timers are used: a *retransmission* timer, a *piggyback* timer and a *crash* timer.

A retransmission timer is started after the *transmission* of a message. If this timer expires before an answer to this message is received, the message is retransmitted.

A piggyback timer is started after the *reception* of a message which has to be answered. If this timer expires before a message is sent back, an acknowledgement message is sent to indicate the correct reception of the message involved and to announce the delay of the answer.

A crash timer is used by a Client to investigate whether a Server is still alive. This timer is started after the reception of the acknowledgement message from the Server. If no new acknowledgement message or a reply message is received before this timer expires, an enquiry message is sent to the Server.

Figure 5.1 shows the state diagrams of the ATP for the Client and the Server, without timers. Sent messages are put in plain text, received messages are put in italics. The initial state and the final state are shaded.

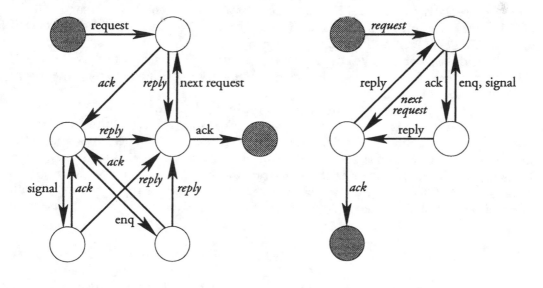

a. *Client process*   b. *Server process*

Figure 5.1   State diagrams of the Amoeba Transaction Protocol

A Client starts a transaction with the transmission of a request to a Server. The Client, now waiting for a reply, starts a retransmission timer. If this timer expires before anything is received from the Server, the request is retransmitted. Retransmission is done a fixed number of times. If nothing is received from the Server after a certain number of retransmissions, the transaction is aborted and the Client is given notice of the transaction failure.

When a Server receives a request, a piggyback timer is started and the Server process starts handling the request. If a reply comes up before the piggyback timer expires, this reply is sent back to the Client. Otherwise an acknowledgement message is sent, indicating the reception of the request.

If the Client receives a reply an acknowledgement message is not sent back immediately. A piggyback timer is started. If a new transaction call to the same Server is issued before this timer expires, the request of the new transaction serves as an acknowledgement. Distinction of consecutive transactions between a Client and a Server is guaranteed by numbering of the messages. In the message header one byte is reserved for this number. The Client uses the same Client transaction record, thus speeding up communications.

Expiration of the piggyback timer of the Client process leads to the transmission of a separate acknowledgement message from the Client to the Server. With this message a (sequence of) transaction(s) is finished and the Client transaction record is deleted.

If the Client receives an acknowledgement of the request a crash timer is started. If this timer expires before a reply message is received an enquiry message is sent from the Client to the Server to investigate whether or not the Server is still alive. A retransmission timer is started. Expiration of this timer before an acknowledgement or a reply is received leads to a retransmission of the enquiry message. After a certain number of retransmissions of the enquiry message the transaction is aborted and the Client is given notice of a Server crash.

When the Server receives an enquiry message a piggyback timer is started. If this timer expires before a reply message is sent, an acknowledgement message is sent to the Client.

When the Server comes up with a reply, it is sent to the Client and a retransmission timer is started. As soon as an acknowledgement of the reception of the reply is received from the Client (this can be an acknowledgement message or the next request) this timer is stopped, the transaction is completed and the Server transaction record is deleted. If the retransmission timer expires the reply is retransmitted. After a certain number of retransmissions of the reply, the transaction is considered completed anyhow, and the Server is informed by the Transaction layer.

As mentioned above, a transaction call blocks the Client process. However, an external interrupt can unblock the Client process. After examining the cause of the interrupt the Client may decide to abort the transaction. It can do so by sending a *signal* message to the Server process involved in the transaction pending. A signal message can be transmitted only when the connection with the Server is established, indicated by the reception of an acknowledgement message from the Server. Note that sending a signal message after the reception of a reply is useless; the transaction has already been completed.

A Server may receive a signal message or ignore it. A Server can react on a received signal message as it likes. However, in all cases the transaction has to be completed by the Server by sending a reply to the Client. The Server is not allowed to stop immediately. The reply, for instance, may contain information about what the Server has done with the signal message.

In the ATP the retransmission of messages requires special attention. A retransmission may be caused by the loss of the original message *or* by the loss of the acknowledgement of the reception of the message. In the second case the receiving process does not expect a retransmission. However, it will have to deal with it. In most cases the message can be received and its contents can be ignored. But sometimes a special action is required: if a Client process does not receive an acknowledgement message after sending a request, it will retransmit the request. When a Server process has received the request and sent an acknowledgement message, it only expects an enquiry message from the Client process. But this message will never be sent by the Client process; after a certain number of retransmissions of the request the Client process will give up, signalling a transaction failure. In order to prevent this 'livelock' the Server process will have to retransmit the acknowledgement message after the reception of a request that has been received before.

Figures 5.2 to 5.5 show some event sequences in the Amoeba Transaction Protocol. The numbers represent the transaction number.

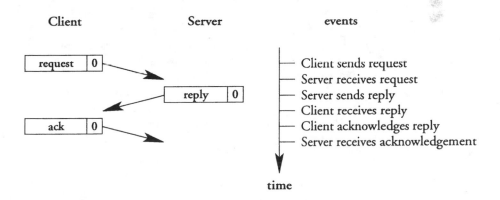

Figure 5.2   A simple transaction

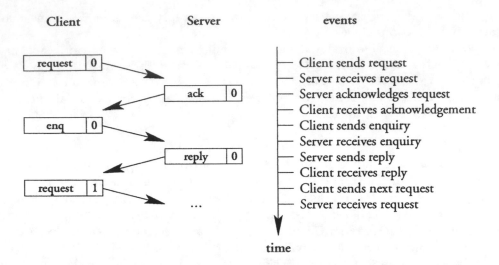

Figure 5.3   A transaction with delayed reply

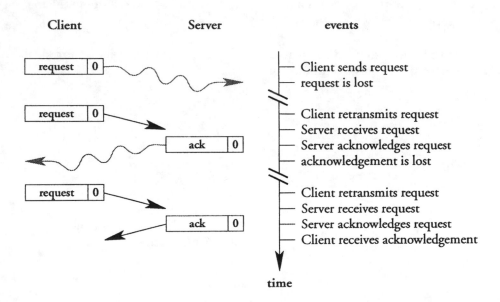

Figure 5.4   A transaction with loss of messages

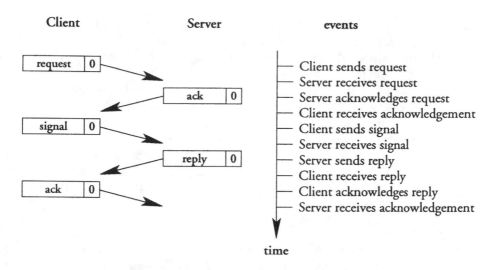

Figure 5.5   A transaction with a signal message

5.3 SPECIFICATION OF THE AMOEBA TRANSACTION PROTOCOL

In the specification of the ATP we will introduce two processes, *CLIENT* and *SERVER*, which generate and consume requests, replies and signals. The two processes, *CLTP* (Client Transaction Protocol) and *SRTP* (Server Transaction Protocol), will take care of the Amoeba Transaction Protocol. The two processes, *CHCS* (Channel from Client to Server) and *CHSC* (Channel from Server to Client) are used to model the communication channels. These processes communicate with each other by ports. It should be clear that these communication ports have nothing to do with the Amoeba 'Port Layer'.

Figure 5.6 shows the names of the ports connecting the different processes.

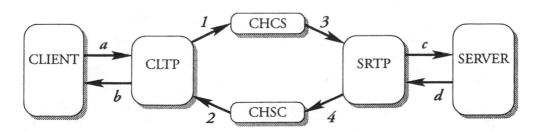

Figure 5.6   Processes and port names

The ATP uses several timers that generate time-outs. In both the *CLTP* process and the *SRTP* process at most one timer is running at a time, so in the implementation of the protocol a single timer can be used. None of the timers need to be very secure, so a 'sweep algorithm' can be used, which periodically polls the state of a process. On entering a certain state a timer is started with a certain value. If after a certain number of polls the state of the process has not changed, a time-out is generated. We will not give a specification of such a sweep algorithm, in the specification of the processes *CLTP* and *SRTP* (sections 5.3.7 and 5.3.8) we will use the atomic actions *rto*, *pto* and *cto* to indicate a retransmission time-out, a piggyback time-out and a crash time-out. The ATP is *not* robust with respect to premature time-outs. This will be explained at the end of section 5.3.8.

In the PSF specification of the ATP we will use several data modules from the standard PSF library: *Booleans*, *Naturals*, *Data* and *Queues*. Besides these modules several data modules are needed that are specific for the ATP.

5.3.1   AMOEBA DATA

The module *Amoeba-data* provides several sorts and functions, used to model the communication between the process pairs *CLIENT - CLTP* and *SERVER - SRTP*. The sort *SIGNAL* is used to model signal parameters in a signal message. The constant *signal* of this sort represents a default signal. The sort *STATUS-REPORT* models Transmission Status Reports from the processes *CLTP/SRTP* to the processes *CLIENT/SERVER*. Three constants are defined, representing a transaction failure, a transaction completion and a server crash.

```
data module Amoeba-data
begin

  exports
    begin
      sorts
        SIGNAL,
        STATUS-REPORT
      functions
        signal   : -> SIGNAL            -- default signal
        tr-fail  : -> STATUS-REPORT     -- transaction failure
        tr-compl : -> STATUS-REPORT     -- transaction completed
        sv-crash : -> STATUS-REPORT     -- server crash
    end

end Amoeba-data
```

5.3.2   MESSAGES

In this protocol three types of messages are distinguished: data messages (requests and replies), signal messages and control messages (enquiries and acknowledgements). Each message contains a header. Requests and replies also contain a data field of variable length. A signal message does not contain a separate data field, free header bytes are used to specify the signal parameters.

A message header contains several fields: a message identification, the message length (only relevant for request and reply messages), a sequence number, destination and reply ports, a signature and a parameter field for higher level use. In the data module *Messages* only two or three of these fields, directly relevant for the Transaction Protocol, are explicitly specified: a message identification and a sequence number. The sort *ID* and the constants *req, rep, sig, enq* and *ack* are used for message identification. The module *Naturals* is imported to provide the sequence numbers. The header function uses the *ID* and *NATURAL* fields, with an optional field for signals. The modules *Data* and *Amoeba-data* are imported to provide the sorts needed.

```
data module  Messages
begin

  exports
    begin
      sorts
        MESSAGE,HEAD,ID
      functions
        defm :                        -> MESSAGE      -- default message
        mess : HEAD # DATA            -> MESSAGE
        mess : HEAD                   -> MESSAGE
        head : ID # NATURAL           -> HEAD
        head : ID # NATURAL # SIGNAL  -> HEAD
        req  :                        -> ID
        rep  :                        -> ID
        sig  :                        -> ID
        enq  :                        -> ID
        ack  :                        -> ID
    end

  imports
    Naturals,Data,Amoeba-data

end Messages
```

5.3.3   MAXIMUM NUMBER OF RETRANSMISSIONS

The data module *MaxRetr* provides a parameter with the constant *max*, the maximum number of retransmissions of a certain message after a time-out. We will suppose that one constant will do for different kinds of messages (requests, replies, signals, enquiries, acknowledgements). This module will be imported by the modules for the processes *CLTP* and *SRTP*. The constant *max* is specified as a parameter, which can be bound to a specific natural number later on.

```
data module  MaxRetr
begin

  parameters
    maxretr
      begin
        functions
          max : -> NATURAL
      end maxretr
```

```
    imports
       Naturals

  end MaxRetr
```

5.3.4 CHANNEL STATES

The channel specification in section 5.3.9 uses several 'channel states'. These states are specified as constants of the sort *CHANNEL-STATE*. The data module *ChannelStates* provides this sort and the channel states *accept*, *deliver* and *lost*.

```
    data module ChannelStates
    begin

      exports
        begin
          sorts
            CHANNEL-STATE
          functions
            accept  : -> CHANNEL-STATE
            deliver : -> CHANNEL-STATE
            lost    : -> CHANNEL-STATE
        end

    end ChannelStates
```

5.3.5 THE CLIENT

We are only interested in Client and Server actions related with the ATP. So we will specify a Client process that can perform a *transaction* call or, after an interrupt during a transaction, can perform a *putsig* call, or ignore the interrupt. In the specification the atomic actions *transaction* and *putsig* are used to model the transaction call and the putsig call, they do not communicate with other actions.

As we are not interested in the actual contents of a request and reply, we will use the default sort *DATA* from the PSF standard library data module *Data* to specify these contents.

After a transaction call a request is sent to the network and the Client process starts waiting for a reply or an error message (transaction failure or Server crash). While waiting an interrupt can come up. The Client process is not bound to send a signal after an interrupt. In this state, by performing a single *skip* action, the process also has the possibility to continue waiting for a reply. If, after an interrupt, a reply or an error message is received before a signal is sent, the interrupt has become useless, because for the Server process the transaction is already completed. So, sending a signal makes no sense.

```
    process module Client
    begin

      exports
        begin
```

```
       atoms
         sa,rb : DATA
         sa     : SIGNAL
         rb     : STATUS-REPORT
       processes
         CLIENT
     end

 imports
   Data,Amoeba-data

 atoms
   transaction : DATA
   interrupt
   putsig       : SIGNAL

 processes
   CLREQ : DATA
   CLREP
   CLSIG : SIGNAL

 variables
   request : -> DATA
   sg       : -> SIGNAL

 definitions
         -- Start of transaction:
   CLIENT = sum(request in DATA, transaction(request).CLREQ(request))

         -- Hand over request to CLTP process:
   CLREQ(request) = sa(request).CLREP

         -- Receive reply or status report ; an interrupt may be
         -- followed by a signal:
   CLREP =
         sum(reply in DATA, rb(reply).CLIENT)
     +   sum(error in STATUS-REPORT, rb(error).CLIENT)
     +   interrupt.
         (   skip.CLREP
          +  skip.sum(sg in SIGNAL,putsig(sg).CLSIG(sg)))

         -- Hand over signal or receive reply or receive status report:
   CLSIG(sg) =
         sa(sg).CLREP
     +   sum(reply in DATA, rb(reply).CLIENT)
     +   sum(error in STATUS-REPORT, rb(error).CLIENT)

 end Client
```

5.3.6   THE SERVER

The Server process starts with a *get request* call to indicate that it is ready to receive
a request. After the reception of a request a reply is produced. As we are not
interested in the contents of the reply an arbitrary reply from the sort *DATA* is sent

back. During the handling of a request a signal message can be received from the Client process. If a signal is received it is up to the Server process to decide what to do. If no signals are wanted (no *getsig* call is issued), the signal will be read, but no special action will follow. When the reception of a signal is 'enabled' the Server may act as it likes. This distinction is not shown in the specification below: a reply is transmitted in any case. After the transmission of a reply the 'transaction completed' status report is awaited from the SRTP process.

In the specification the atomic actions *getreq* and *putrep* are used to model the get request call and the put reply call, they do not communicate with other actions.

```
process module Server
begin

  exports
    begin
      atoms
        sd,rc : DATA
        rc    : SIGNAL
        rc    : STATUS-REPORT
      processes
        SERVER
    end

  imports
    Data,Amoeba-data

  atoms
    getreq
    putrep : DATA

  processes
    SRON,SRREQ,SRTRC
    SRREP : DATA

  variables
    reply : -> DATA
    sg    : -> SIGNAL

  definitions
          -- Start listening for a request:
    SERVER = getreq.SRON

          -- Receive request:
    SRON = sum(request in DATA, rc(request).SRREQ)

          -- Produce reply or read signal:
    SRREQ =
        sum(reply in DATA, putrep(reply).SRREP(reply))
      + sum(sg in SIGNAL, rc(sg).SRREQ)

          -- Hand over reply to SRTP process or read signal:
    SRREP(reply) =
        sd(reply).SRTRC
      + sum(sg in SIGNAL, rc(sg).SRREP(reply))
```

```
                -- Wait for transaction completion:
        SRTRC = rc(tr-compl).SERVER

    end Server
```

5.3.7   THE TRANSACTION PROTOCOL - THE CLIENT PART

The process *CLTP* gets a request from the CLIENT process and takes care of a reliable handling of the Client part of a transaction. A transaction ends with the reception of a reply from a Server, followed by an acknowledgement message or the next request from the Client to the same Server. For the distinction of consecutive requests a *sequence number* is used (*seq-nr* in the specification below). Detected errors can lead to a premature end of a transaction. Such errors can be a *transaction failure* (no Server is found to handle the request) or a *server crash* (the connected Server does not respond any more). Errors are reported to the Client process.

As discussed earlier, three possible time-outs are used by the CLTP process: *rto* (retransmission time-out), *cto* (crash time-out) and *pto* (piggyback time-out). These time-outs are represented by atomic actions in the CLTP process. The process variable *nr-retr* is used to count the number of retransmissions of a particular message. If *nr-retr* reaches a certain maximum an error is reported. This maximum is derived from the imported data module *MaxRetr*.

After the transmission of a request with a sequence number greater than zero the CLTP process can receive a reply on the previous request. This can happen because in the ATP the Client process supposes that a transmitted request, serving as an acknowledgement for a previous transaction, will arrive safely at the Server process. If this is not the case the Server will retransmit the reply. After reading this reply it can be ignored; the retransmission timer of the CLTP process will initiate a retransmission of the request, if necessary. After the reception of an acknowledgement message from the Server we are sure that the request has arrived, so no previous replies will arrive any more.

The CLTP process can receive a signal from the Client process in one state only: while waiting for a reply or a crash time-out. This state corresponds with the sub-process *CTACK* in the specification below.

```
    process module Cltp
    begin

        exports
          begin
            atoms
                ra,sb : DATA
                ra    : SIGNAL
                sb    : STATUS-REPORT
                s1,r2 : MESSAGE
            processes
                CLTP
          end
```

```
imports
  Amoeba-data,MaxRetr,Messages

atoms
  rto,pto,cto

processes
  CTREQ,CTREQREP              : DATA # NATURAL # NATURAL
  CTACK,CTREPWAIT,CTREPACK : NATURAL
  CTENQ,CTENQREP             : NATURAL # NATURAL
  CTREP                      : DATA # NATURAL
  CTSIG,CTSIGREP             : SIGNAL # NATURAL # NATURAL
  CTERR                      : STATUS-REPORT

variables
  request,reply : -> DATA
  seq-nr,nr-retr          : -> NATURAL
  sg            : -> SIGNAL
  error         : -> STATUS-REPORT

definitions
        -- Read first request from Client:
  CLTP = sum(request in DATA, ra(request).CTREQ(request,zero,zero))

        -- (Re)send request to Server:
  CTREQ(request,seq-nr,nr-retr) =
        s1(mess(head(req,seq-nr),request)).
            CTREQREP(request,seq-nr,nr-retr)

        -- Read reply, previous reply, ack from Server or
        -- retransmission time-out for request:
  CTREQREP(request,seq-nr,nr-retr) =
        sum(reply in DATA,r2(mess(head(rep,seq-nr),reply)).
            CTREP(reply,seq-nr))
    + [gt(seq-nr,zero) = true] ->
            sum(reply in DATA, r2(mess(head(rep,dec(seq-nr)),reply)).
              CTREQREP(request,seq-nr,nr-retr))
    + r2(mess(head(ack,seq-nr))).CTACK(seq-nr)
    + rto.(   [lt(nr-retr,max) = true] ->
                  CTREQ(request,seq-nr,inc(nr-retr))
          + [lt(nr-retr,max) = false] ->
                  CTERR(tr-fail))

        -- Read reply from Server or read signal from Client or
        -- crash time-out for Server reply:
  CTACK(seq-nr) =
        sum(reply in DATA, r2(mess(head(rep,seq-nr),reply)).
            CTREP(reply,seq-nr))
    + sum(sg in SIGNAL, ra(sg).CTSIG(sg,seq-nr,zero))
    + cto.CTENQ(seq-nr,zero)

        -- (Re)send enquiry to Server:
  CTENQ(seq-nr,nr-retr) =
        s1(mess(head(enq,seq-nr))).CTENQREP(seq-nr,nr-retr)
```

```
                -- Read reply, ack from Server or
                -- retransmission time-out for enquiry:
        CTENQREP(seq-nr,nr-retr) =
            sum(reply in DATA, r2(mess(head(rep,seq-nr),reply)).
                CTREP(reply,seq-nr))
          + r2(mess(head(ack,seq-nr))).CTACK(seq-nr)
          + rto.(    [lt(nr-retr,max) = true] ->
                        CTENQ(seq-nr,inc(nr-retr))
                  + [lt(nr-retr,max) = false] ->
                        CTERR(sv-crash))

                -- Send reply to Client:
        CTREP(reply,seq-nr) = sb(reply).CTREPWAIT(seq-nr)

                -- Read next request from Client or read reply from Server
                -- (again) or piggyback time-out for acknowledgement:
        CTREPWAIT(seq-nr) =
            sum(request in DATA, ra(request).
                CTREQ(request,inc(seq-nr),zero))
          + sum(reply in DATA,r2(mess(head(rep,seq-nr),reply)).
                CTREPWAIT(seq-nr))
          + pto.CTREPACK(seq-nr)

                -- Send acknowledgement to Server, transaction is completed:
        CTREPACK(seq-nr) = s1(mess(head(ack,seq-nr))).CLTP

                -- (Re)send signal to Server:
        CTSIG(sg,seq-nr,nr-retr) =
            s1(mess(head(sig,seq-nr,sg))).CTSIGREP(sg,seq-nr,nr-retr)

                -- Read reply, ack from Server or retransmission time-out for
                -- signal:
        CTSIGREP(sg,seq-nr,nr-retr) =
            sum(reply in DATA, r2(mess(head(rep,seq-nr),reply)).
                CTREP(reply,seq-nr))
          + r2(mess(head(ack,seq-nr))).CTACK(seq-nr)
          + rto.(    [lt(nr-retr,max) = true] ->
                        CTSIG(sg,seq-nr,inc(nr-retr))
                  + [lt(nr-retr,max) = false] ->
                        CTERR(sv-crash))

                -- Send error message to Client, transaction is finished:
        CTERR(error) = sb(error).CLTP

    end Cltp
```

5.3.8   THE TRANSACTION PROTOCOL - THE SERVER PART

The process *SRTP* handles the Server part of the Amoeba Transaction Protocol. A received request is sent to the SERVER process. If this process is not ready to accept the request (no *getreq* call has been made), the communication between the SRTP process and the SERVER process will fail. In this state the SRTP process reads a retransmitted request without doing anything.

If the SERVER process has accepted the request, but no reply has come up within a certain time (indicated by a piggyback time-out), an acknowledgement message is sent to the Client. As explained in section 5.2.1 the reception of an 'old' request leads to the retransmission of the acknowledgement message.

The reception of an enquiry message from the Client will also lead to the transmission of an acknowledgement message (if the reply has not come in between). When the SERVER process produces a reply it is sent to the Client and the SRTP process starts waiting for a reaction: an acknowledgement message or a next request. As long as no reaction is received a piggyback time-out generates (a finite number of) retransmissions of the reply. After a certain number of retransmissions the SRTP process gives up and the SERVER process is notified that the transaction is completed. When a reaction (an acknowledgement or a consecutive request) is received the SERVER process gets the same status report.

After the transmission of an acknowledgement message a signal message can arrive. This signal is always handed over to the SERVER process, which has to decide whether it is willing to react on signals or not. The SRTP process just continues waiting for a reply from the SERVER process.

As in the CLTP process, the process variables *seq-nr* and *nr-retr* are used to indicate the sequence number of a transaction and the number of retransmissions of a certain message.

```
process module Srtp
begin

  exports
    begin
    atoms
      sc,rd : DATA
      sc    : SIGNAL
      sc    : STATUS-REPORT
      r3,s4 : MESSAGE
    processes
      SRTP
  end

  imports
    Amoeba-data,MaxRetr,Messages

  atoms
    rto,pto

  processes
    STREQ,STNEXTREQ     : DATA # NATURAL
    STREPWAIT,STSENDACK : NATURAL
    STREP,STACKWAIT     : DATA # NATURAL # NATURAL
    STACK
    STSIG               : SIGNAL # NATURAL

  variables
    request,reply : -> DATA
    seq-nr,nr-retr : -> NATURAL
    sg             : -> SIGNAL
```

```
definitions
        -- Read first request:
 SRTP = sum(request in DATA, r3(mess(head(req,zero),request))).
           STREQ(request,zero))

        -- Send request to Server or read request again from Client:
 STREQ(request,seq-nr) =
        sc(request).STREPWAIT(seq-nr)
    +   sum(request1 in DATA, r3(mess(head(req,seq-nr),request1))).
           STREQ(request,seq-nr))

        -- Read reply from Server or read signal, request (again),
        -- enquiry from Client or piggyback time-out:
 STREPWAIT(seq-nr) =
        sum(reply in DATA, rd(reply).STREP(reply,seq-nr,zero))
    +   sum(sg in SIGNAL, r3(mess(head(sig,seq-nr,sg)))).
           STSIG(sg,seq-nr))
    +   sum(request in DATA,r3(mess(head(req,seq-nr),request))).
           STREPWAIT(seq-nr))
    +   r3(mess(head(enq,seq-nr))).STREPWAIT(seq-nr)
    +   pto.STSENDACK(seq-nr)

        -- Send acknowledgement to Client:
 STSENDACK(seq-nr) = s4(mess(head(ack,seq-nr))).STREPWAIT(seq-nr)

        -- (Re)send reply to Client:
 STREP(reply,seq-nr,nr-retr) = s4(mess(head(rep,seq-nr),reply)).
           STACKWAIT(reply,seq-nr,nr-retr)

        -- Read next request, acknowledgement, enquiry, previous
        -- request or signal from Client ; retransmission time-out for
        -- reply:
 STACKWAIT(reply,seq-nr,nr-retr) =
        sum(request in DATA, r3(mess(head(req,inc(seq-nr)),request))).
           STNEXTREQ(request,inc(seq-nr)))
    +   r3(mess(head(ack,seq-nr))).STACK
    +   r3(mess(head(enq,seq-nr))).STACKWAIT(reply,seq-nr,nr-retr)
    +   sum(request in DATA, r3(mess(head(req,seq-nr),request)))).
           STACKWAIT(reply,seq-nr,nr-retr)
    +   sum(sg in SIGNAL,r3(mess(head(sig,seq-nr,sg))))).
           STACKWAIT(reply,seq-nr,nr-retr)
    +   rto.(   [lt(nr-retr,max) = true] ->
                    STREP(reply,seq-nr,inc(nr-retr))
            +   [lt(nr-retr,max) = false] ->
                    STACK)

        -- Report 'transaction completed' to Server and continue with
        -- next request:
 STNEXTREQ(request,seq-nr) = sc(tr-compl).STREQ(request,seq-nr)

        -- Report 'transaction completed' to Server:
 STACK = sc(tr-compl).SRTP

        -- Send signal to Server:
 STSIG(sg,seq-nr) = sc(sg).STREPWAIT(seq-nr)
end Srtp
```

It should be noticed that the ATP is not robust with respect to premature time-outs. An example will illustrate this. Suppose that the retransmission timer of the SRTP process uses a very short time interval compared to the same timer of the CLTP process. Now it is possible that, after *max* retransmissions of a reply on a first request, the SRTP process decides that the transaction is completed and goes to the initial state. If the SRTP process now receives a request with sequence number zero, it is not able to tell if this message is a retransmitted request or a new request. So the ATP is only correct if the various timer intervals are tailored to each other.

5.3.9   THE CHANNELS

As explained in section 5.2 different messages are used by the ATP: requests, replies, signals, enquiries and acknowledgements, each with a sequence number. In order to simplify the specification of the channel processes we will suppose that both channels can transport messages of the same kind, although the channel from Server to Client will actually never transport a signal message or an enquiry message.

The ATP performs no special actions on the reception of damaged messages. So we will introduce a simple channel process in which a message is transported correctly from the entrance port to the exit port, or gets lost.

We will specify a channel as an infinite queue that is always able to accept a message or (if the queue is not empty) to deliver a message. We will give only the specification of the channel process *CHCS* from Client to Server. The specification of the other channel process, *CHSC*, is the same, besides port names, process names and the name of the atom *lost-cs* (which is changed into *lost-sc*) .

In the specification the data modules *ChannelStates* (see section 5.3.4) and *Queues* (from the PSF standard library) are imported. The parameter sort *Q-ELEMENT* is bound to *MESSAGE*, the parameter constant *default-q-element* is bound to *defm*. In order to emphasise the use of this queue, the sort *QUEUE* is renamed to *CHANNEL* and the constant *empty-queue* is renamed to *empty-channel*.

```
process module  Chcs
begin

   exports
     begin
       atoms
         r1,s3 : MESSAGE
         lost-cs
       processes
         CHCS
     end

   imports
     Queues{Queue-parameter bound by [Q-ELEMENT -> MESSAGE,
         default-q-element -> defm] to Messages
         renamed by [QUEUE -> CHANNEL, empty-queue -> empty-channel]},
     ChannelStates

   processes
     CHCS  : CHANNEL # CHANNEL-STATE
```

```
variables
  cq : -> CHANNEL

definitions
          -- Initialization with empty channel; channel state = accept:
  CHCS = CHCS(empty-channel,accept)

          -- Read a message or make a non-deterministic choice
          -- between the two output-alternatives:
  CHCS(cq,accept) =
          sum(m in MESSAGE,  r1(m).CHCS(enqueue(m,cq),accept))
      +   [eq(length(cq),zero) = false] ->
              (   skip.CHCS(cq,deliver)
              +   skip.CHCS(cq,lost))

          -- Read a message or deliver a message:
  CHCS(cq,deliver) =
          sum(m in MESSAGE,  r1(m).CHCS(enqueue(m,cq),deliver))
      +   s3(serve(cq)).CHCS(dequeue(cq),accept)

          -- Read a message or lose a message:
  CHCS(cq,lost) =
          sum(m in MESSAGE,  r1(m).CHCS(enqueue(m,cq),lost))
      +   lost-cs.CHCS(dequeue(cq),accept)

end Chcs
```

Note: it would have been possible to specify one generic channel process and to create the two 'physical' channel processes by a double import with parameter binding and renamings, as in chapter 4. However, in the asymmetrical setting of the ATP with two different sides (Client and Server) we have chosen to use two separate channel specifications. One of these specifications has been shown.

5.3.10   THE AMOEBA TRANSACTION PROTOCOL

A specification of the ATP as a whole consists of the encapsulated merge of the four processes *CLTP, SRTP, CHCS* and *CHSC*. Besides the definition of the process *ATP* this module contains the definitions of the encapsulation set *H1* and the communications over the ports 1-4.

```
process module Atp
begin

  exports
    begin
      atoms
        c1,c2,c3,c4 : MESSAGE
      processes
        ATP
    end

  imports
    Cltp,Srtp,Chcs,Chsc
```

```
sets of atoms
   H1 = {r1(m),s1(m),r2(m),s2(m),r3(m),s3(m),r4(m),s4(m)  |
         m in MESSAGE}

communications
   s1(m)|r1(m) = c1(m) for m in MESSAGE
   s2(m)|r2(m) = c2(m) for m in MESSAGE
   s3(m)|r3(m) = c3(m) for m in MESSAGE
   s4(m)|r4(m) = c4(m) for m in MESSAGE

definitions
   ATP = encaps(H1, CLTP || SRTP || CHCS || CHSC)

end Atp
```

5.3.11   THE COMMUNICATION BETWEEN CLIENT AND SERVER

Finally the communication between Client and Server by means of the Amoeba
Transaction Protocol can be specified in a process *Communication*: the encapsulated
merge of the processes *CLIENT, ATP* and *SERVER*.

```
process module Communication
begin

   exports
     begin
       atoms
         ca,cb,cc,cd : DATA
         ca,cc       : SIGNAL
         cb,cc       : STATUS-REPORT
       processes
         COMMUNICATION
     end

   imports
     Client,Atp,Server

   sets of atoms
      H2 =   {sa(d),ra(d),sb(d),rb(d),sc(d),rc(d),sd(d),rd(d) |d in DATA}
           + {sa(s),ra(s),sc(s),rc(s) |s in SIGNAL}
           + {sb(e),rb(e),sc(e),rc(e) |e in STATUS-REPORT}

   communications
      sa(d)|ra(d) = ca(d) for d in  DATA
      sb(d)|rb(d) = cb(d) for d in  DATA
      sc(d)|rc(d) = cc(d) for d in  DATA
      sd(d)|rd(d) = cd(d) for d in  DATA
      sa(s)|ra(s) = ca(s) for s in  SIGNAL
      sc(s)|rc(s) = cc(s) for s in  SIGNAL
      sb(e)|rb(e) = cb(e) for e in  STATUS-REPORT
      sc(e)|rc(e) = cc(e) for e in  STATUS-REPORT

   definitions
      COMMUNICATION = encaps(H2, CLIENT || ATP || SERVER )

end Communication
```

This specification can be made concrete by importing it into a new process module and by binding the parameters from the modules *Data* and *MaxRetr* to actual sorts and constants.

5.4 SUMMARY

The Amoeba Transaction Protocol is used for short interactions between a Client process and a Server process in the Amoeba Distributed Operating System. A basic transaction consists of three messages: the Client sends a request to the Server, the Server responds with a reply and the Client acknowledges this reply. If a transaction is (almost) immediately followed by another one between the same Client and Server, the request of the consecutive transaction functions serves as an acknowledgement of the reply. A Client may interrupt the handling of a request by sending a signal message to the Server. A Server is not obliged to react to this message; in any case it has to send a reply to the Client.

The reliability of the Transaction Protocol is enhanced by the use of additional control messages (enquiry messages, acknowledgement messages) and several timers.

The Amoeba Transaction Protocol does not fit in the ISO OSI reference model. In section 5.2 some attention is paid to the model that underlies this protocol.

5.5 BIBLIOGRAPHICAL NOTES

The Amoeba Distributed Operating System, including the protocol specified in this chapter, is described in the Ph.D. Thesis of Mullender ([Mul85]). In [Mul90] an ACP specification and a verification of a slightly different version of the Amoeba Transaction Protocol are given. In this text an error in the original ATP of Mullender is mentioned: the absence of a Server reaction on an already received request. The specification in this chapter does not contain this error.

In [Bru91b] the Amoeba Transaction Protocol is specified in both ACP and PSF. This text has been used as the basis for this chapter.

CHAPTER 6
TWO SIMPLE PROTOCOLS FOR LOCAL AREA NETWORKS

J.J. BRUNEKREEF

6.1 INTRODUCTION

In a Local Area Network (LAN) different stations are connected by one single physical medium (the channel), organized as a *bus* or a *ring*, see Figure 6.1.

Each station uses the medium for transmitting data to and receiving data from the other stations. A problem arises when more than one station wants to use the medium for transmission at the same time. Different data streams will interfere with each other, if no measures are taken to regulate the use of the medium.

Such a *collision* can be avoided if not more than one station on the network is permitted to use the medium for transmission at a time. This restriction can be implemented by using a *token*: a special permission for transmission. If only one token exists in a network only one station (the token-holder) can transmit at a certain moment, all other stations will have to wait until they hold the token. Rules will be necessary to determine how long each station is allowed to hold the token and which station becomes the next token-holder. A protocol that is based on token passing is usually called a *Token Bus* protocol or a *Token Ring* protocol, according to the logical network structure.

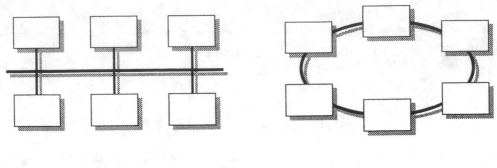

a. Stations connected by a bus   *b. Stations connected by a ring*

Figure 6.1   Network configurations

A second approach to avoiding a collision is based on *carrier sensing*; a station can see if another station is transmitting by watching the medium. As long as the medium is in use (the carrier signal is *on*), the station refrains from transmitting. Using carrier sensing, a collision may still occur if two or more stations start transmitting at (almost) the same time. When a collision is detected all receiving stations have to throw away what they have received so far. All transmitting stations will have to stop transmitting and, after some time, retransmit the same message. If every station waits the same time interval, the same collision will occur again (and again). Therefore the waiting time is usually determined by a choice from a bounded time interval. A protocol for a multi-access channel that is based on collision detection by carrier sensing is called a *CSMA/CD* protocol: Carrier Sense Multiple Access with Collision Detection.

In general a CSMA/CD protocol performs very well when the network is not heavily loaded or when in general only one station is transmitting. In those situations very few collisions will occur. Almost every message can be transmitted without delay. However, when many stations are frequently transmitting to the network, the performance of a CSMA/CD protocol goes down significantly. A lot of collisions and resulting retransmissions can bring the network throughput to very low figures.

A Token Ring or Token Bus protocol performs very well on a heavily loaded network. A token in the network will be captured almost immediately by a station that is waiting for it, so the usage of the network bandwidth will be close to optimal. But when there is not much traffic in the network, the token passing mechanism will lead to a significant delay: if a station that wants to transmit a message has just missed the token it will have to wait for the token to pass by again, although the network probably is idling during the whole waiting period.

In this chapter two simple LAN protocols are introduced and specified. The first one uses a token in a ring-shaped network, the second one is based on carrier sensing in a network that uses a bus. We will call the first protocol *STR* (Simple Token Ring), the second one *SEN* (Simple *Ethernet*, the most well-known *CSMA/CD* protocol).

The two protocols provide a basic level of understanding of the mechanisms involved, thus serving as an introduction to the 'real-life' Token Ring and Ethernet protocols as described in the official IEEE standards.

Preceding the specification of the two protocols, in section 6.2 we will specify a general interface to the layer situated above this type of protocols, the *Logical Link Control* layer. The sections 6.3 and 6.4 are devoted to the *STR* and *SEN* protocols.

6.2   THE LOGICAL LINK CONTROL INTERFACE

6.2.1   GENERAL DESCRIPTION

Protocols for Local Area Networks are situated in the Data Link layer and the Physical layer of the ISO OSI reference model. However, they do not provide a complete data link service to higher layers, because no acknowledgement service or connection oriented service is offered. Therefore, an additional sub-layer is defined for LANs: the *Logical Link Control* (LLC) sub-layer, officially standardized by the IEEE. Different LAN protocols use the same interface to the LLC sub-layer, so only one LLC sub-layer protocol is needed. The part of the Data Link layer that is covered by the LAN protocols is usually called the *Media Access Control* (MAC) sub-layer. The name of the sub-layer indicates the primary concern of this part of the LAN protocols: getting access to a medium that is used by multiple stations.

Figure 6.2 shows the positioning of LAN protocols in the OSI network hierarchy. The LLC sub-layer is serviced by one of the LAN protocols: Token Ring, CSMA/CD or another protocol.

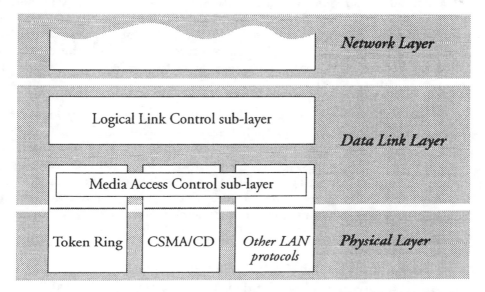

Figure 6.2   LAN protocols and the ISO OSI network hierarchy

We will define a simple interface between the protocols specified here and a Logical Link Control sub-layer, based on OSI-like *service primitives*. Service primitives can be regarded as a kind of procedure call, generated by a (sub-)layer process for communication between adjacent (sub-)layer processes.

The following service primitives are introduced: *request* (a request to transmit data), *indication* (an indication that relevant data have come in from the medium) and *confirmation* (a confirmation of a transmission).

Below, each primitive is defined, together with its parameters, generating entity and effect.

* request (destination_address, data_unit)

This service primitive is generated by the LLC sub-layer to tell the LAN protocol that data have to be transmitted to a station, indicated by the *destination_address*. The data are packed together in a so called *data_unit*. After generation of this primitive the LAN protocol will create a *frame* by adding some information to the data unit (for example a destination address and a source address) and transport the frame via the medium to the LLC sub-layer of another station on the network, indicated by the destination_address parameter.

* indication (source_address, data_unit)

This service primitive is generated by the LAN protocol to indicate to the LLC sub-layer the reception of a frame from another station. The *source_address* parameter indicates the origin of the frame. The *data_unit* parameter specifies the data received in the frame. Only the contents of a frame with the appropriate destination address are delivered to the LLC sub-layer.

* confirmation (transmission_status)

This service primitive is generated by the LAN protocol to tell the LLC sub-layer whether the handling of a request call was successful or not, as far as can be observed from the transmitting station. The parameter can have two values: *tr-succeeded* (transmission succeeded) or *tr-failed* (transmission failed). A successful transmission does not imply that the data unit has been received correctly by the destination station. It is up to the LLC sub-layer or higher levels to decide what to do when a transmission has failed.

As we shall see in the coming sections LAN protocols are primarily focussed on getting access to the medium (the channel) and, in the case of a CSMA/CD protocol, scheduling retransmissions in the case of a detected collision. A LAN protocol does not provide any form of error recovery or separate acknowledgement service.

In sections 6.3 and 6.4 we will give a formal specification of the two simple LAN protocols STR and SEN. In the remainder of this section we will give a specification of the LLC sub-layer, focussed on the interface between this sub-layer process and the LAN protocols.

6.2.2   A SPECIFICATION OF THE LLC INTERFACE

The process *LLC(s)* serves as a specification of the interface-part of the LLC sub-layer to the MAC sub-layer for a specific station *s*. So only the following actions are relevant:

- perform a request call = transmit data to another station
- get an indication call = receive data from another station
- get a confirmation call = receive a confirmation (about the handling of a request) from the local MAC process

Any other action of the LLC(s) process is not relevant to the LLC-MAC interface and will not be specified.

Figure 6.3 shows the LLC(s) actions involved with the communication between this process and the MAC sub-layer. The direction of the arrows indicates the initiating component: a request is generated by the LLC process, a confirmation or an indication is generated by the MAC process.

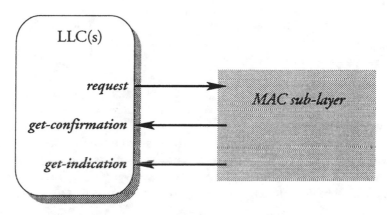

Figure 6.3   LLC(s) actions involved with the communication with the MAC sub-layer

Before we give a specification of the LLC, we introduce two modules with general network information. These modules, *Network-data* and *Network-parameters*, will be used throughout this chapter.

6.2.2.1   Network Data

In the data module *Network-data* the PSF standard library module *Naturals* is imported for the station numbers. These numbers are used to identify the atoms and processes of a particular station *s*. In the specification the first parameter of an atom or a process always indicates the station number. The sort *ADDRESS* and the functions *addr* and *eq* are specified for the destination address in a request and the source address in an indication. The function *addr* maps a station number on a station address. So the address of a station *s* is *addr(s)*. This function makes specific address constants superfluous. The function *eq* provides an equality test on addresses.

```
data module  Network-data
begin

   exports
     begin
       sorts
         ADDRESS
       functions
         addr            : NATURAL              -> ADDRESS
         eq              : ADDRESS # ADDRESS -> BOOLEAN
     end

   imports
     Naturals

   variables
     sn1,sn2 : -> NATURAL

   equations
     [1]  eq(addr(sn1),addr(sn2)) = eq(sn1,sn2)

end Network-data
```

6.2.2.2 Network Parameters

In the process module *Network-parameters* two sets are specified as parameters. The set *SN-set* contains the set of station numbers in a network. The set *ADDR-set* contains the set of station addresses in a network. By binding these parameters to concrete sets, a concrete network can be specified.

```
process module  Network-parameters
begin

   parameters
     Network-parameters
        begin
          sets of NATURAL
              SN-set
            of ADDRESS
              ADDR-set
        end Network-parameters

   imports
     Network-data

end Network-parameters
```

6.2.2.3 LLC Data

The data module *LLC-data* provides the sort *TR-STATUS*. The constants *tr-failed* and *tr-succeeded* of the sort *TR-STATUS* model the status messages transmission failed and transmission succeeded.

```
data module LLC-data
begin

  exports
    begin
      sorts
        TR-STATUS
      functions
        tr-failed    : -> TR-STATUS
        tr-succeeded : -> TR-STATUS
    end

end LLC-data
```

6.2.2.4   The Logical Link Control Interface

The LLC(s) process is split up into two separate processes: *LLCR(s)* and *LLCI(s)*. The first process generates a request and waits for a confirmation. The second process waits for an indication. The LLC(s) process is specified as the merge (and not as the sum) of the processes LLCR(s) and LLCI(s) because otherwise the sending part, waiting for a confirmation, would block the receiving of an indication.

The sort *DATA* from the imported PSF standard library module *Data* is used to specify the contents of a data unit of a request or an indication.

The following abbreviations are used in the specification:

s = station number
da = destination address
du = data unit
rsa = received source address
rdu = received data unit
rts = received transmission status

```
process module LLC
begin

  exports
    begin
      atoms
        request         : NATURAL # ADDRESS # DATA
        get-confirmation : NATURAL # TR-STATUS
        get-indication  : NATURAL # ADDRESS # DATA
      processes
        LLC : NATURAL
    end

  imports
    Network-parameters,LLC-data,Data

  processes
    LLCR : NATURAL
    LLCI : NATURAL
    LLCC : NATURAL
```

```
variables
  s : -> SN-set

definitions
        -- Generate a request:
  LLCR(s) =
        sum(da in ADDR-set, sum(du in DATA,request(s,da,du).LLCC(s)))

        -- After a request a confirmation is expected:
  LLCC(s) = sum(rts in TR-STATUS, get-confirmation(s,rts).LLCR(s))

        -- Wait for an indication:
  LLCI(s) =
        sum(rsa in ADDR-set, sum(rdu in DATA,
           get-indication(s,rsa,rdu).LLCI(s)))

        -- The LLC process:
  LLC(s) = LLCR(s)||LLCI(s)

end LLC
```

The communication between the LLC(s) process and STR(s) / SEN(s) processes will be specified in the following sections.

6.3   A SIMPLE TOKEN RING PROTOCOL: STR

6.3.1   GENERAL DESCRIPTION

A Token Ring protocol defines a medium access mechanism for a ring-shaped network, based on token passing. A ring-shaped network can be regarded as a collection of point-to-point connections between neighbour stations. Each station has to deal with two communication links, with its neighbours in the ring. We will use a *unidirectional* ring, on which only one-way traffic is possible. A station transmits in the direction of its 'successor' and receives from its 'predecessor' in the ring.

In order to avoid collisions, a *token* travels around the ring. When a station captures the token it has the permission to use the medium for transmission. In the STR protocol, after the transmission of a frame, the station is obliged to pass the token to its successor in the ring, in order to guarantee that every station gets its turn. After some time the station will receive the token again from its predecessor, after which a next frame can be transmitted. When no frame is waiting for transmission the token is passed immediately.

When a station receives a frame, it copies the entire frame into an internal buffer. When the destination address in the frame is equal to the station's network address, the data part is delivered to the LLC sub-layer, together with the source address of the data. A received frame is always transmitted to the successor station. It is the responsibility of the *transmitting* station to remove a frame from the ring, thus preventing a frame from travelling around the ring forever. This means that, when a station is receiving, all incoming information is copied to the outgoing line. (However, as we shall see later on, sometimes a field is changed.) While transmitting, the incoming information is not copied to the ring. When the transmission of a frame is finished the token is sent to the successor in the ring.

In the STR protocol we will define two transmission formats: one for the token and one for data frames. In these formats we will abstract from physical aspects such as synchronization between stations and focus completely on the logical aspects.

A token consists of one field, the *Access Control* field (*AC*). A data frame consists of five fields. The control field *AC'* holds the token, modified by the transmitting station, so no other station will recognize it as a token. The *DA* and *SA* fields contain the *Destination Address* and the *Source Address*. The *DU* field contains the *data unit* that has to be transmitted. We will not put any constraints on the length of this field. LANs usually have a very low error rate, so very long frames are not considered a problem. The *Transmission Status* field (*TS*) is set to the initial value *tr-failed* (transmission failed) by the transmitting station, it is modified by the station addressed to the value *tr-succeeded* (transmission succeeded).
Figure 6.4 shows the two formats.

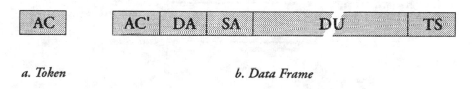

| *a. Token* | *b. Data Frame* |

Figure 6.4   Transmission formats in the STR protocol

When a station has a frame to transmit it waits for the token. When the token is received the *AC* field is modified, so the next station on the ring will not recognize the token and start transmitting too. After the modified *AC* field the *DA*, *SA*, *DU* and *TS* fields are transmitted.

When a station in the ring goes down it still has to perform an elementary *by-pass* function: received tokens or frames have to be transmitted to the successor in the ring, otherwise the ring is 'broken' and the protocol will fail. Sending a frame to a station that is down will result in a negative confirmation at the transmitting station. In the coming sections we will also specify the by-pass mode for a station.

6.3.2   A SPECIFICATION OF THE STR PROTOCOL

We will specify a process *STR(s)*, performing the STR protocol actions for a single station *s*. Figure 6.5 shows the STR(s) actions involved with the communication between this process and the LLC(s) process. The direction of an arrow indicates the initiating component. Resulting communications are listed above the arrows. Read and write actions are part of the communications between adjacent STR processes in the ring.

In the specification of the STR(s) process we will suppose that the token or a data frame is transmitted or received as a whole, not bit-by-bit. This abstraction surely is a violation of reality: the length of a LAN ring is usually not more than a few hundreds of meters and transmission rates are high (megabits per second), so only a few bits can be 'in the channel' at the same time. However, in this simple protocol we will continue to follow the chosen approach of abstraction from physical details and focus on the logical essentials of a Token Ring protocol, even if this does not conform to reality.

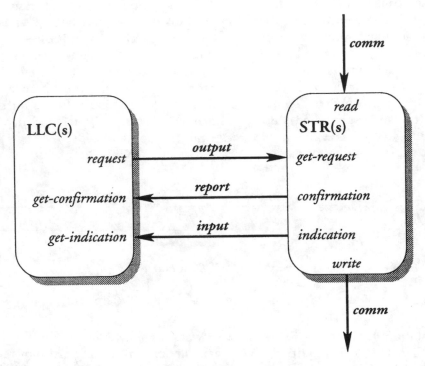

Figure 6.5   Communications between the LLC(s) process and the STR(s) process

6.3.2.1 STR Data

The data module *STR-data* contains the sorts and functions that are specific for the STR protocol. This module provides the sort *MODE* with the constants *normal* and *bypass*. The parameter *nr-stations* with the constant *nrs* of the sort *NATURAL* determines the number of stations in the ring. The function *next* determines the successor of a station in the ring. The function *next* is defined as *next(s) = (s + 1) mod nrs*. The parameter constant *nrs* can be bound later on.

```
data module STR-data
begin

   parameters
     nr-stations
       begin
         functions
           nrs : -> NATURAL   -- Number of stations in the ring
       end nr-stations
```

```
exports
  begin
    sorts
      MODE
    functions
      normal :          -> MODE
      bypass :          -> MODE
      next   : NATURAL -> NATURAL
  end

imports
  Naturals

variables
  sn : -> NATURAL

equations
  [1]  next(sn) = mod(inc(sn),nrs)

end STR-data
```

6.3.2.2 Frames

The data module *Frames* is used to specify the messages (frames) of the STR protocol. Specified are the sort *ACCESS-CONTROL* with the constants *token* and *non-token* and the sort *FRAME* with the function *frame* (to construct a token frame or a data frame).

```
data module Frames
begin

  exports
    begin
      sorts
        ACCESS-CONTROL,FRAME
      functions
        token     : -> ACCESS-CONTROL
        non-token : -> ACCESS-CONTROL     -- the modified token
        frame     : ACCESS-CONTROL  -> FRAME
        frame     : ACCESS-CONTROL # ADDRESS # ADDRESS # DATA # TR-STATUS
                    -> FRAME
    end

  imports
    Network-data,LLC-data,STR-data,Data

end Frames
```

6.3.2.3 The Simple Token Ring Protocol

As mentioned above, a station that is down still has to perform some elementary network functions. Therefore we will specify two modes of operation for the STR(s) process: *normal* and *bypass*. We will not go into the network management details that cause a change from one mode to the other. A change is possible by a non-deterministic choice in the STR(s) process below.

In the normal operation mode the STR process starts with waiting for a request call to come in from the local LLC(s) process or a token or a data frame to come in from the ring. When a request is received the process has to wait for the token to pass by. As soon as the token is captured, a data frame is transmitted to the successor in the ring and, after some time, received back from the predecessor and removed from the ring. The frame status field is inspected, results are reported to the LLC(s) process by a confirmation call. Afterwards the token is passed to the successor in the ring. If the token is received without any data waiting for transmission it is passed to the successor in the ring immediately.

When a frame is received, the destination address is inspected. If it is the station address the relevant parts of it (the source address, the data unit) are delivered to the LLC(s) process by an indication call. A frame is transmitted with the Transmission Status field set to 'trf' (transmission failed). If the destination address is recognized the TS field of the frame is modified to 'trs' (transmission succeeded) in order to provide the transmitting station with some information on the success of the transmission of the frame. A received frame is sent to the successor in the ring, until it reaches the station that transmitted the frame. This station removes the frame from the ring and transmits the token to its successor. A station that transmits a frame to itself will not get an indication call from its protocol layer, the confirmation call will report a transmission failure.

As the channels between the different stations are supposed to be short and error-free we will not give a separate specification of the medium behaviour. We will directly define the communication between two neighbour STR processes as the communication between a write action of a process and a read action of its successor in the ring. So a *write(s,...)* action communicates with a *read(next(s),...)* action.

In the by-pass mode a message that is received is passed to the successor in the ring without inspecting the contents of the message.

Most of the abbreviations used in the specification of the STR(s) process have been introduced in section 6.2. In addition the following abbreviations are used:

    md = operation mode
    sa = source address
    rda = received destination address
    ts = transmission status

The process module *Network-parameters* is imported for the sets *SN-set* and *ADDR-set*.

```
process module STR
begin

  exports
    begin
      atoms
        get-request  : NATURAL # ADDRESS # DATA
        confirmation : NATURAL # TR-STATUS
        indication   : NATURAL # ADDRESS # DATA
```

```
        read            : NATURAL # FRAME
        write           : NATURAL # FRAME
        comm            : NATURAL # FRAME
     processes
        STR : NATURAL
   end
```

imports
  Network-parameters,Frames

processes
```
  STR    : NATURAL # MODE
  REQ    : NATURAL # ADDRESS # DATA
  TRANSM : NATURAL # ADDRESS # DATA
  TOKEN  : NATURAL
  RECM   : NATURAL
  IND    : NATURAL # ADDRESS # DATA
  COPY   : NATURAL # ADDRESS # ADDRESS # DATA # TR-STATUS
```

communications
  write(s,m)|read(next(s),m) = comm(s,m) **for** s **in** NATURAL, m **in** FRAME

variables
```
  s     : -> SN-set
  da,sa : -> ADDR-set
  du    : -> DATA
  ts    : -> TR-STATUS
  bm    : -> FRAME
```

definitions
```
        -- First the mode of operation is chosen:
  STR(s) = sum(md in MODE, skip.STR(s,md))
```

```
        -- In the normal mode the STR process starts with waiting for a
        -- request, the token or an incoming frame:
  STR(s,normal) =
       sum(da in ADDR-set, sum(du in DATA,get-request(s,da,du).
          REQ(s,da,du)))
    +  read(s,frame(token)).TOKEN(s)
    +  RECM(s).STR(s)
```

```
        -- A request has been received, wait for the token or an
        -- incoming frame:
  REQ(s,da,du) =
       read(s,frame(token)).TRANSM(s,da,du)
    +  RECM(s).REQ(s,da,du)
```

```
        -- Transmit a data frame and, after the return of the frame,
        -- deliver a confirmation:
  TRANSM(s,da,du) =
       write(s,frame(non-token,da,addr(s),du,tr-failed)).
          sum(rda in ADDR-set, sum(rsa in ADDR-set,
          sum(rdu in DATA, sum(rts in TR-STATUS,
          read(s,frame(non-token,rda,rsa,rdu,rts)).
          confirmation(s,rts).TOKEN(s)))))
```

```
                     -- Transmit the token:
      TOKEN(s) = write(s,frame(token)).STR(s)

                     -- Test the destination address of an incoming frame:
      RECM(s) =
            sum(rda in ADDR-set, sum(rsa in ADDR-set, sum(rdu in DATA,
               sum(rts in TR-STATUS,
               read(s,frame(non-token,rda,rsa,rdu,rts)).
               (   [eq(rda,addr(s)) = true] -> IND(s,rsa,rdu)
                +  [eq(rda,addr(s)) = false] -> COPY(s,rda,rsa,rdu,rts))
               ))))

                     -- Handle a received frame with destination address equal to
                     -- station address:
      IND(s,sa,du) = indication(s,sa,du).
                  write(s,frame(non-token,addr(s),sa,du,tr-succeeded))

                     -- Handle a received frame with destination address not equal
                     -- to station address:
      COPY(s,da,sa,du,ts) = write(s,frame(non-token,da,sa,du,ts))

                     -- In the by-pass mode messages are passed to the successor in
                     -- the ring only:
      STR(s,bypass) = sum(bm in FRAME,read(s,bm).write(s,bm).STR(s))

   end STR
```

6.3.2.4 The Simple Token Ring Network

Now the Simple Token Ring network is defined as the encapsulated merge of the STR(s) processes with s an element of *SN-set*.

In order to start the token passing on the ring the action *write(dec(nrs),token)* is added to the merge, so initially station number 0, the successor of station number *dec(nrs)* will receive the token.

```
   process module  STRnetwork
   begin

     exports
       begin
         processes
           STRnetwork
       end

     imports
       STR

     sets of atoms
         H = {write(s,m),read(s,m) | s in SN-set, m in FRAME}

     definitions
       STRnetwork = encaps(H, write(dec(nrs),frame(token)) ||
             merge(s in SN-set, STR(s)))

   end STRnetwork
```

6.3.2.5   A Simple Token Ring Station

Finally we will specify a process *STRstation(s)*, which defines the interaction between the LLC process and the STR process. It is defined as the encapsulated merge of the two processes *LLC(s)* and *STR(s)*.

```
process module STRstation
begin

  exports
    begin
      atoms
        output : NATURAL # ADDRESS # DATA
        report : NATURAL # TR-STATUS
        input  : NATURAL # ADDRESS # DATA
      processes
        STRstation : NATURAL
    end

  imports
    LLC, STR

  sets of atoms
    H1 = {request(s,da,du),get-request(s,da,du),confirmation(s,ts),
          get-confirmation(s,ts),indication(s,sa,du),
          get-indication(s,sa,du) | s in SN-set, da in ADDR-set,
          sa in ADDR-set, du in DATA, ts in TR-STATUS }

  communications
    request(s,da,du)|get-request(s,da,du) = output(s,da,du)
        for s in SN-set, da in ADDR-set, du in DATA
    confirmation(s,ts)|get-confirmation(s,ts) = report(s,ts)
        for s in SN-set, ts in TR-STATUS
    indication(s,sa,du)|get-indication(s,sa,du) = input(s,sa,du)
        for s in SN-set, sa in ADDR-set, du in DATA

  variables
    s : -> SN-set

  definitions
    STRstation(s) = encaps(H1, LLC(s) || STR(s) )

end STRstation
```

The specification can be tailored to a specific network by importing the modules *STRnetwork* or *STRstation* into a new process module and by binding the parameters *Network-parameters* and *nr-stations* to the specific network constants. The parameter *Data* will also have to be bound.

6.4   A SIMPLE CSMA/CD PROTOCOL: SEN

6.4.1   GENERAL DESCRIPTION

In this section we will look at a simple protocol for a multi-access channel, based on carrier sensing and collision detection. We will call the protocol the *Simple Ethernet* (SEN) protocol, because it is a simplified version of the most widely known real-life CSMA/CD protocol.

We will suppose a network configuration consisting of a bus and n stations connected with the bus. Each station can transmit to and receive from each other station in the network. When two or more stations use the medium (the bus) for transmission at the same time, a *collision* occurs and messages are garbled. In this case, each transmitting station has to retransmit its message after a certain time. For proper operation a network station can perform two 'functions' on the medium: *carrier sensing* (to see if the medium is free or in use) and *collision detection* (to see if more than one station is transmitting).

In the SEN protocol we will define two transmission formats, a *data frame* and a *jam frame*. As in the STR protocol we will abstract from physical aspects like synchronization and we will focus on the logical operation.

A data frame consists of three fields: the DA and SA fields contain the *Destination Address* and the *Source Address*. The DU field contains the *Data Unit* that has to be transmitted. The length of the DU field is not determined. A jam frame consists of three fields too. The first two fields are equal to the corresponding fields of the data frame, the *JAM* field contains a *Jam Signal*. The use of this signal will be explained below. Figure 6.6 shows the formats.

a. Data Frame   *b. Jam Frame*

Figure 6.6   Transmission format of a data frame and a jam frame in the SEN protocol

In a real-life CSMA/CD protocol a frame is transmitted bit by bit. The carrier sense and collision detection functions can be performed before and after each bit-transmission or bit-reception. For reasons of simplicity we will not specify a bitwise transmission in the SEN protocol. However, a framewise transmission (as in the STR protocol) will not work out fine: during the transmission of a frame a collision may come up, which has to be noticed by the transmitting station. Therefore, we will split a frame into two parts at the transmitting side and take such a part as a transmission unit. The first part contains the *DA* and *SA* fields, the second part contains the *DU* or *JAM* field.

When a station wants to transmit a data unit (a *request* is generated by the LLC sub-layer, see section 6.2), the first part of the frame is transmitted if the medium is idle. We will suppose that, once a first frame part has been transmitted, all stations can see that the medium is in use and thus will refrain from sending. So a collision (due to transmissions of other stations) will appear before this moment, it will not emerge afterwards. After the transmission of the first frame part, the carrier is sensed again by the transmitting station. If no collision has come up the second part of the data frame is transmitted and the transmission is regarded as successful. If a collision is detected a *jam signal* is transmitted instead of the second part of a data frame. This signal is meant to garble all information on the medium, so all stations will receive a garbled frame.

After the transmission of a jam signal a station waits some time before a frame is retransmitted. Different stations will have to wait different time intervals, otherwise the same collision will occur again. In the SEN protocol we will use a simple algorithm to determine the waiting time. We will put an upper limit, *maxrt*, to the number of retransmissions. If after *maxrt* retransmissions another collision occurs, the transmission fails.

The (un)successful transmission of a frame is notified to the LLC sub-layer by the *confirmation* service primitive.

A station continuously waits for an incoming frame. As soon as a frame is received it is inspected. If a valid frame is received the destination address is inspected and, if this address is equal to the station address, the relevant frame parts are transferred to the LLC sub-layer of a station by the *indication* service primitive. An invalid (garbled) frame is rejected.

6.4.2   A SPECIFICATION OF THE SEN PROTOCOL

The SEN protocol communicates with the same LLC process as the STR protocol. The interface between the protocol and the LLC sub-layer consists of three communications (*output*, *report* and *input*), initiated by the service primitives *request*, *confirmation* and *indication*. The specification of the LLC process was given in section 6.2.

The protocol actions for a network station *s* will be performed by the process *SEN(s)*. In the SEN protocol we will have to be aware of the fact that different stations can transmit to the medium at the same time, so a frame can come in at any time, even while the station is transmitting. Therefore, we will split the SEN(s) process into two separate parallel processes: *TRANSM(s)* for the transmitting part and *REC(s)* for the receiving part.

In a CSMA/CD protocol the medium behaviour is a complex process. Different stations can transmit frames simultaneously and transmitted frames and carrier status functions have to be presented to all the network stations. In section 6.4.2.6 we will introduce a separate process *MEDIUM* to specify the medium behaviour. This process serves as a model of the transmission medium between the different network stations in the SEN protocol. Most abbreviations used in the specification of the SEN protocol have already been introduced in sections 6.2 and 6.3.

Figure 6.7 shows the interfaces between the processes *LLC(s)*, *TRANSM(s)*, *REC(s)* and *MEDIUM* with the actions and resulting communications.

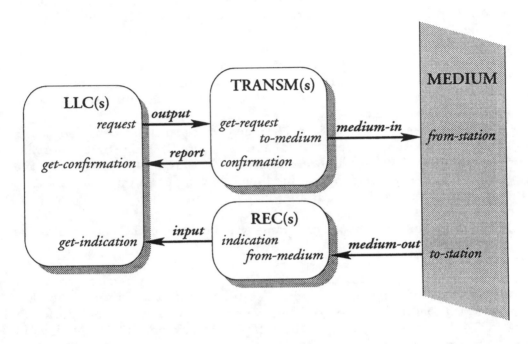

Figure 6.7   Communications between the processes

6.4.2.1 SEN Data

The data module *SEN-data* contains the sorts and functions that are specific to the SEN protocol. This module defines only the parameter *nr-retr* which represents the constant *maxrt*, the maximum number of retransmissions after a collision.

```
data module SEN-data
begin

  parameters
    nr-retr
      begin
        functions
          maxrt : -> NATURAL
      end nr-retr

  imports
    Naturals

end SEN-data
```

6.4.2.2 Frames

The data module *Frames* exports two sorts: *FRAME* for the different messages on the medium and *MEDIUM-STATUS* for medium status values. The functions *frame-1*, *frame-2* and *frame* serve as constructors of (parts of) data frames. The boolean function *is-garbled-frame* tests if a message is equal to the constant *garbled-frame*. The constant *jam* denotes the jam signal. Three constants are defined for the sort *MEDIUM-STATUS*: *idle, on* and *collision*. The medium status is *idle* when no station is transmitting. The medium status is *on* when a single station is transmitting. The medium status is *collision* when two or more stations are transmitting at the same time.

```
data module  Frames
begin

   exports
     begin
       sorts
         FRAME,MEDIUM-STATUS
       functions
         frame            : ADDRESS # ADDRESS # DATA -> FRAME
         frame-1          : ADDRESS # ADDRESS       -> FRAME
         frame-2          : DATA                     -> FRAME
         jam              :                          -> FRAME
         garbled-frame    :                          -> FRAME
         is-garbled-frame : FRAME                    -> BOOLEAN
         idle             :                          -> MEDIUM-STATUS
         on               :                          -> MEDIUM-STATUS
         collision        :                          -> MEDIUM-STATUS
     end

   imports
     Network-data,Data

   variables
     da,sa : -> ADDRESS
     du    : -> DATA

   equations
     [1]  is-garbled-frame(garbled-frame) = true
     [2]  is-garbled-frame(frame(da,sa,du)) = false
          --for reasons of completeness only :
     [3]  is-garbled-frame(frame-1(da,sa)) = true
     [4]  is-garbled-frame(frame-2(du)) = true
     [5]  is-garbled-frame(jam) = true

end Frames
```

6.4.2.3 The Simple Ethernet Protocol - Transmitting Part

In the TRANSM(s) and REC(s) processes, carrier sensing, collision detection and data transfer is done in one single communication action. For instance, in the TRANSM(s) process the action *to-medium(s,idle,frame-1(da,addr(s)))* can only communicate with the action *from-station(s,idle,frame-1(da,sa))* from the MEDIUM process, which guarantees that the first frame part is transmitted to the medium only when the medium is idle. So the medium status parameter in these atomic actions serves a synchronization purpose.

The TRANSM(s) process starts by waiting for a request from the LLC sub-layer. When a request arrives, the first frame part, with the DA and SA fields, is sent to the medium if the medium is idle. After the transmission of the first part the medium status determines what will happen next. If the carrier sense signal is 'on' (no collision), a second frame part with the data unit is transmitted. If a collision is detected, a jam signal is transmitted instead.

When the transmission of a frame has succeeded, the LLC(s) process is notified by the *confirmation* service primitive with the parameter set to *tr-succeeded* (transmission succeeded).

After a collision the TRANSM(s) process waits a number of periods before the frame is retransmitted. The atomic action *wait* represents a wait for one period. In the SEN protocol the number of waiting periods is chosen equal to the station number *s*: a simple way to assure that no two stations will wait the same time interval. If after *maxrt* retransmissions another collision occurs, the SEN protocol gives up. The LLC level is notified of this excessive collision by the *confirmation* service primitive with the parameter set to *tr-failed* (transmission failed).

The parameter *n* is used in the process equations to count the number of retransmissions of a frame after a collision has been detected. The process module *Network-parameters* is imported for the sets *SN-set* and *ADDR-set*.

```
process module Transmit
begin

   exports
     begin
       atoms
         get-request  : NATURAL # ADDRESS # DATA
         confirmation : NATURAL # TR-STATUS
         to-medium    : NATURAL # MEDIUM-STATUS # FRAME
         wait
       processes
         TRANSM : NATURAL
     end

   imports
     Network-parameters,LLC-data,SEN-data,Frames

   processes
     TRF1   : NATURAL # ADDRESS # DATA # NATURAL
     TRF2   : NATURAL # ADDRESS # DATA # NATURAL
     COLL   : NATURAL # ADDRESS # DATA # NATURAL
     TRWAIT : NATURAL # NATURAL # ADDRESS # DATA # NATURAL

   variables
     s,w : -> SN-set
     n   : -> NATURAL
     da  : -> ADDRESS
     du  : -> DATA
```

```
definitions
          -- Start with waiting for a request:
   TRANSM(s) =
          sum(da in ADDR-set,sum(du in DATA, get-request(s,da,du).
             TRF1(s,da,du,zero)))

          -- Transmit the first part of the frame if the medium is
          -- idle:
   TRF1(s,da,du,n) = to-medium(s,idle,frame-1(da,addr(s))).
             TRF2(s,da,du,n)

          -- Transmit data unit or jam signal, dependent on medium
          -- status:
   TRF2(s,da,du,n) =
          to-medium(s,on,frame-2(du)).confirmation(s,tr-succeeded).
             TRANSM(s)
     +    to-medium(s,collision,jam).COLL(s,da,du,n)

          -- Test on excessive collision:
   COLL(s,da,du,n) =
          [lt(n,maxrt) = true ] -> TRWAIT(s,zero,da,du,n)
     +    [lt(n,maxrt) = false] -> confirmation(s,tr-failed).TRANSM(s)

          -- Wait 'w' periods after a collision before retransmitting a
          -- frame:
   TRWAIT(s,w,da,du,n) =
          [eq(w,s) = true ] -> TRF1(s,da,du,inc(n))
     +    [eq(w,s) = false] -> wait.TRWAIT(s,inc(w),da,du,n)

end Transmit
```

6.4.2.4 The Simple Ethernet Protocol - Receiving Part

The process *REC(s)* continuously waits for a frame to arrive. There is no need to perform a function on a frame part. So, for reasons of simplicity, a frame comes in as a whole, not split up in two parts. A received frame is inspected whether it is correct or garbled (due to a collision). A garbled frame is rejected. A correct frame is inspected. If the destination address is equal to the station address the data unit and the source address from the frame are delivered to the LLC(s) process by the indication service primitive. Otherwise the frame is rejected.

```
process module  Receive
begin

   exports
     begin
       atoms
         indication  : NATURAL # ADDRESS # DATA
         from-medium : NATURAL # MEDIUM-STATUS # FRAME
       processes
         REC : NATURAL
     end
```

```
imports
  Network-parameters,Frames

variables
  s : -> SN-set

definitions
          -- Wait for incoming frame, check frame:
  REC(s) =
          from-medium(s,on,garbled-frame).REC(s)
      +   sum(rda in ADDR-set,sum(rsa in ADDR-set,sum(rdu in DATA,
            from-medium(s,on,frame(rda,rsa,rdu)).
            (    [eq(rda,addr(s)) = true ] ->
                    indication(s,rsa,rdu).REC(s)
            +   [eq(rda,addr(s)) = false] ->
                    REC(s) ) )))

end Receive
```

6.4.2.5 The Simple Ethernet Protocol

The SEN protocol for a network station *s* (the SEN(s) process) is specified by the merge of the processes *TRANSM(s)* and *REC(s)*:

```
process module SEN
begin

  exports
    begin
      processes
        SEN : NATURAL
    end

  imports
    Transmit,Receive

  variables
    s : -> SN-set

  definitions
    SEN(s) = TRANSM(s) || REC(s)

end SEN
```

6.4.2.6 The Medium

Now we will turn to the process *MEDIUM*, representing the physical transmission medium between the network stations (the bus). It should be clear that this process is not meant as a general specification of a multi-access medium, it is meant to service the Transmit and Receive processes of the network stations in the SEN protocol, as specified above.

The MEDIUM process has to accept inputs (parts of frames), transmitted by network stations and deliver a frame and a medium status to all stations. If two or more stations are transmitting at the same moment, a collision has to be detected and reported. By admitting more than one input action before an output action is executed, the possibility of a collision is created.

A merge of the send actions *to-station* for a frame guarantees that a frame is delivered to *every* station, so it can never be missed by a single station.

In the case of a collision the number of transmitted frames that caused the collision is counted by the process parameter *c*. A collision is resolved after all these *c* stations have transmitted a jam signal. After a collision a garbled frame is presented to all stations.

```
process module Medium
begin

  exports
    begin
      atoms
        from-station : NATURAL # MEDIUM-STATUS # FRAME
        to-station   : NATURAL # MEDIUM-STATUS # FRAME
      processes
        MEDIUM
    end

  imports
    Frames,Network-parameters

  processes
    MEDF  : NATURAL # ADDRESS # ADDRESS
    MEDFD : ADDRESS # ADDRESS # DATA
    MEDC  : NATURAL
    MEDCR : NATURAL

  variables
    s,c   : -> SN-set
    da,sa : -> ADDR-set
    du    : -> DATA

  definitions
        -- Start the medium in idle state, wait for a frame to come in:
    MEDIUM = sum(s in SN-set,sum(da in ADDR-set,sum(sa in ADDR-set,
          from-station(s,idle,frame-1(da,sa)).MEDF(s,da,sa))))

        -- The medium holds a single frame part. Receive a second frame
        -- part or receive a first frame part from another station:
    MEDF(s,da,sa) =
        sum(du in DATA, from-station(s,on,frame-2(du)).
          MEDFD(da,sa,du))
      + sum(s1 in SN-set,sum(da1 in ADDR-set,sum(sa1 in ADDR-set,
          from-station(s1,idle,frame-1(da1,sa1)).MEDC(s(s(zero))))))

        -- Deliver a correct frame to all stations:
    MEDFD(da,sa,du) =
        merge(s in SN-set, to-station(s,on,frame(da,sa,du))).MEDIUM
```

```
                 -- The medium holds more than one frame. Receive a jam signal
                 -- or a first frame part from another station:
     MEDC(c) =
             sum(s in SN-set, from-station(s,collision,jam).MEDCR(dec(c)))
         +   sum(s1 in SN-set,sum(da1 in ADDR-set,sum(sa1 in ADDR-set,
                 from-station(s1,idle,frame-1(da1,sa1)).MEDC(inc(c)))))

                 -- A collision is resolved if the medium has received a jam
                 -- signal from all c stations:
     MEDCR(c) =
             [eq(c,zero) = true] ->
                 merge(s in SN-set, to-station(s,on,garbled-frame)).MEDIUM
         +   [eq(c,zero) = false] ->
                 sum(s in SN-set, from-station(s,collision,jam).
                     MEDCR(dec(c)) )


     end Medium
```

6.4.2.7 The Simple Ethernet Network

The Simple Ethernet Network is defined as the encapsulated merge of the SEN(s) processes and the Medium process, with *s* an element of *SN-set*.

```
     process module  SENnetwork
     begin

        exports
          begin
            atoms
              medium-in  : NATURAL # MEDIUM-STATUS # FRAME
              medium-out : NATURAL # MEDIUM-STATUS # FRAME
            processes
              SENnetwork
          end

        imports
          SEN,Medium

        sets of atoms
          H = {to-medium(s,ms,m),from-station(s,ms,m),from-medium(s,ms,m),
               to-station(s,ms,m) | s in SN-set, ms in MEDIUM-STATUS,
               m in FRAME}

        communications
          to-medium(s,ms,m)|from-station(s,ms,m) = medium-out(s,ms,m)
              for s in SN-set, ms in MEDIUM-STATUS, m in FRAME
          from-medium(s,ms,m)|to-station(s,ms,m) = medium-in(s,ms,m)
              for s in SN-set, ms in MEDIUM-STATUS, m in FRAME

        definitions
          SENnetwork = encaps(H, merge(s in SN-set, SEN(s)) || MEDIUM)

     end SENnetwork
```

6.4.2.8 A Simple Ethernet Station

As for the Simple Token Ring Protocol, we will specify a process *SENstation(s)*, which defines the interaction between the LLC process and the SEN process. It is defined as the encapsulated merge of the two processes *LLC(s)* and *SEN(s)*. Due to the uniform interface between our protocols and the LLC sub-layer, this process module only differs from the one in section 6.3.2.5 in the substitution of *SEN* for *STR*.

```
process module SENstation
begin

  exports
    begin
      atoms
        output : NATURAL # ADDRESS # DATA
        report : NATURAL # TR-STATUS
        input  : NATURAL # ADDRESS # DATA
      processes
        SENstation : NATURAL
    end

  imports
    LLC, SEN

  sets of atoms
    H1 = {request(s,da,du),get-request(s,da,du),confirmation(s,ts),
          get-confirmation(s,ts),indication(s,sa,du),
          get-indication(s,sa,du) | s in SN-set, da in ADDR-set,
          sa in ADDR-set, du in DATA, ts in TR-STATUS }

  communications
    request(s,da,du)|get-request(s,da,du) = output(s,da,du)
        for s in SN-set, da in ADDR-set, du in DATA
    confirmation(s,ts)|get-confirmation(s,ts) = report(s,ts)
        for s in SN-set, ts in TR-STATUS
    indication(s,sa,du)|get-indication(s,sa,du) = input(s,sa,du)
        for s in SN-set, sa in ADDR-set, du in DATA

  variables
    s : -> SN-set

  definitions
    SENstation(s) = encaps(H1, LLC(s) || SEN(s) )

end SENstation
```

The specification can be tailored to a specific network by importing the modules *SENnetwork* or *SENstation* into a new process module and by binding the parameters *Network-parameters* and *nr-retr* to specific network constants. The parameter *Data* will also have to be bound.

6.5 SUMMARY

LAN protocols are used for communications in Local Area Networks. In this type of networks a single transmission medium (a bus, a ring) is used by all stations. A problem arises at the moment that more than one station wants to use the medium at the same time. A LAN protocol tries to solve this problem. In practice different solutions are known: a token travelling around a ring and collision detection.

The two simple protocols in this chapter give a basic insight into the principles that underlie the IEEE Token Ring protocol and the IEEE Ethernet protocol. The protocols in this chapter are rather crude simplifications of reality. They are meant to provide a basic level of understanding of the IEEE protocols, without getting confused by all the technical details of an official industrial standard.

The Simple Token Ring protocol shows how access to a ring is regulated by means of token passing. A station that wants to transmit a frame waits until it captures the token. After transmission of the frame the token is passed to the successor in the ring. If a station has no frame to transmit the token is passed immediately.

The Simple Ethernet protocol shows how access to a bus is regulated by means of carrier sensing and collision detection. Before transmitting a frame the carrier (the bus) is sensed. If the carrier is idle the first part of the frame is sent. Afterwards the carrier is sensed again. If no collision has occurred (no other station has started the transmission of a frame), the second part of the frame is transmitted. If a collision is detected, a so called jam signal is transmitted, which tells other stations to throw away what they have received until then. After a collision a station waits a certain time interval before it retransmits a frame.

Preceding the specification of the two protocols, a general interface to this kind of protocol is specified by introducing a Logical Link Control level with a single interface to both LAN protocols.

The PSF specifications of the Simple Token Ring protocol and the Logical Link Control process are rather straightforward. In the specification of the Simple Ethernet protocol the Medium process requires special attention. In PSF only binary communications between processes can be specified; the broadcast of a message over a bus and collision detection on a bus do not fit in with this scheme. So the specification of the Medium process is not really simple.

6.6 BIBLIOGRAPHICAL NOTES

The IEEE standards for the LLC-layer, the Token Ring protocol and the Ethernet protocol can be found in [IEEE85a,b,c]. In [Bru91c] the simple protocols of this chapter are specified in both ACP and PSF. This text has been used as the basis for this chapter.

CHAPTER 7
THE TOKEN RING PROTOCOL

H. JACOBSSON & S. MAUW

7.1 INTRODUCTION

This case study is a formal description of a protocol for a local area network, using the specification language PSF.

One approach to local networking is the ring network. Although various types of rings have been proposed and built, we will study one of the more popular organizations, the *token ring* network. In such a network, a *token* circulates around the ring, which can be captured by one of the components. The component guarding the token is allowed to transmit a message.

The protocol specified in this paper is based on the token ring described in [IEEE85b] as an IEEE standard. This description is given partly in informal, natural language and drawings, and partly by means of state transition systems. The intention of this chapter is to apply a Formal Description Technique in order to give a formal specification of the protocol. In contrast to the protocols in the previous chapters, we try to provide a specification, that resembles an existing standard as much as possible.

7.2 TOKEN RING NETWORK, AN INTRODUCTION

A ring consists of a collection of *ring interfaces* connected by point-to-point links that form a circle, as shown in Figure 7.1. Point-to-point links involve a well-understood and field-proven technology. Due to the sequential ordering of the stations attached to a ring, a ring-based protocol is in general *fair* in the sense that each station eventually will get control of the ring. In a token ring, each station has a known upper bound on channel access. The ring network standardized in [IEEE85b] is called a *token ring* and in this section we will take a closer look on what this is.

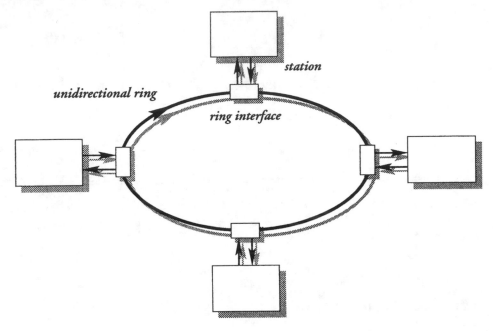

Figure 7.1   A token ring

As mentioned above, a token ring consists of a collection of ring-interfaces connected by point-to-point lines. When a bit arrives at a ring-interface it is copied into a 1-bit buffer and then put into the ring again. While in the buffer, the bit can be inspected and possibly modified before being written out into the ring again. This copying step introduces a 1-bit delay at each ring-interface. A ring-interface is capable of receiving data from its station that is to be transmitted to another station, and it can send data which is addressed to its station, copied from the ring.

In a token ring a special bit pattern, called the *token*, circulates around the ring whenever all stations are idle. When the network is brought up, this bit pattern is inserted only once into the ring. When a station wants to transmit a frame, it has to seize the token and remove it from the ring before transmitting.

Having seized the token, the potential sender knows that no other ring-interface will be able to find the token, let alone capture it, so it is now free to put its message into the ring without the risk of interference with other messages. Collisions between transmissions do not occur since only one station at a time can hold the token and transmit data.

One implication of the token ring design is that the ring itself must have a sufficient delay to contain a complete token, to circulate when all stations are idle. The delay has two components: the 1-bit delay introduced by each station, and the signal propagation delay. In this specification we will not worry about the signal propagation delay and only require that the token ring is started up with enough stations.

Ring-interfaces have two modes of operation, *listen* and *transmit* mode. See Figure 7.2. In the listen mode, the input bits are simply copied to the output. In the transmit mode the ring-interface breaks the connection between input and output and puts its own data onto the ring. This mode is entered only after the token has been seized.

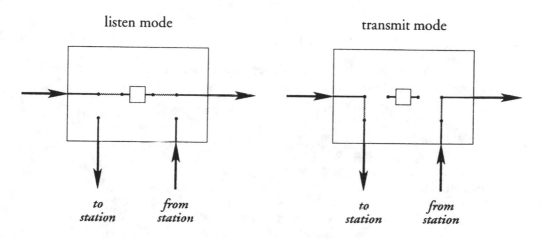

Figure 7.2   A ring-interface
(*adapted from Tanenbaum89*)

After having seized the token and having sent a frame, the sending ring-interface waits for the frame to come back, which will happen after the bits have propagated around the ring once. The receiver has just copied the bits, so the frame is still circulating. The sending ring-interface is the one to remove it from the ring, possibly after comparing it with the original data. This ring architecture puts no limit to the size of the frames, because the entire frame never needs to appear on the ring at one instant.

After a station has finished transmitting the last bit of its frame, it regenerates the token. When the last bit of the frame has gone around and come back, it must be removed, and the ring-interface must switch back into listen mode immediately. This is to avoid the removal of the token that might follow if no other station has seized it.

It is straightforward to handle *acknowledgements* on a token ring. The frame format need only include a 1-bit field for acknowledgements, initially set to zero. When the destination station has received a frame, it needs only to invert the bit, while the rest of the frame remains unmodified.

When traffic is light, the token will spend most of its time circulating idly around the ring. Occasionally a station will seize it, transmit a frame, and regenerate the token afterwards. However, when the traffic is heavy, such that there is a queue of data at each station, most of the time data frames circulate. As soon as a station finishes its transmission and regenerates the token, the next station downstream will see and remove the token. In this manner the permission to send rotates smoothly around the ring, in a round-robin fashion.

Each ring has a *monitor station*, which oversees the ring and is responsible for the correct operation of the ring. Among the monitor's responsibilities are the following: seeing that the token is not lost, taking action when the ring breaks and cleaning the ring up when garbled frames appear.

7.3 SPECIFICATION OF A TOKEN RING

This specification covers only the basic functions defined in the standard, the following parts are omitted:

- priority operation for ring access
- broadcasting by group addressing
- ring maintenance by a monitor station
- (recovering from) error situations
- use of timers

The specification is based on bytes and it assumes that the point-to-point links between the different ring stations are error free. The formats used in the specification are somewhat different from the official standard. These simplifications do not degenerate the network facilities more than is mentioned above. The use of bytes instead of bits can be considered more an abstraction than a simplification.

In the specification *octets* are used as the smallest data item sent around the ring when processes are communicating with each other. An octet is constructed of eight *symbols* in the same manner as 8 bits make a byte. The difference is that a symbol can represent four values: *0, 1, J,* or *K.* The advantage of octets is that special symbols can be used for control functions, such as the starting and the ending of a data frame. The user is allowed to use only bytes and can therefore never generate an ending delimiter by accident or some other essential control symbol. The mapping between bits and symbols is :

0	binary zero bit
1	binary one bit
J	non data but must be interpreted as a binary one bit
K	non data but must be interpreted as a binary zero bit

There are two basic formats used in the specification. The token format (Figure 7.3) follows the IEEE standard but the frame format (Figure 7.4) is slightly simplified. In the frame format two fields are omitted; one for defining frame-types and another for the frame-check sequence, since they play no role in this specification. Other fields are simplified. The following two formats are used:

Figure 7.3   Token format

Figure 7.4   Frame format

SD   Starting Delimiter, 1 octet
AC   Access Control, 1 octet
DA   Destination Address, 1 octet
SA   Source Address, 1 octet
SDU   Service Data Unit, 0 or more octets
ED   Ending Delimiter, 1 octet
FS   Frame Status, 1 octet

A token starts with a starting delimiter, which is used for synchronization of the network and indicates the arrival of information. The access control octet contains a bit, which is called the *token symbol*. The token symbol in the access control field of a token is a zero bit. The ending delimiter marks the end of a transmission.

A frame also starts with a starting delimiter and an access control field. The token symbol in this field is a one bit. The destination and source addresses both consist of only one octet. A service data unit is the information to be transmitted to the receiver's station. It may have arbitrary length. After this, an ending delimiter is transmitted, which indicates the completion of the message. The frame status can be used to acknowledge the arrival of the message at the receiver.

When a station, with a Protocol Data Unit (*PDU*) to transmit, detects the token it changes the token to a start-of-frame sequence and transmits the PDU. The frame status octet is set by the destination station when a frame has been fully copied.

Inherent in this token ring specification is that the ring itself must have at least four ring-interfaces. When all stations are idle, that is when in listen mode, the ring must allow a complete token to circulate on the ring. Hence each station has an implicit buffer of one octet.

7.4   THE SPECIFICATION

The following two sections contain the actual PSF specification of the token ring protocol as described above. The first section covers the data types and the second is about the processes involved in the token ring protocol.

7.4.1   DATA SPECIFICATION

This section contains the specification of the data types necessary for the token ring specification. The various exported sorts and functions in the different data types are all imported in the data module *Utilities*. By definition all the imported functions and sorts are automatically exported in *Utilities*, thus the visible signature is extended with the visible signature of data modules that are being imported. Knowing this, *Utilities* is used later on as the entry-point to all the visible sorts and functions in the part of specification defining the process.

7.4.1.1 Bytes

An element of the sort *BYTE* is constructed from eight bits, using the *byte* constructor. The module *Bits* is imported from the standard library.

```
data module Bytes
begin

  exports
    begin
      sorts
        BYTE
      functions
        byte : BIT # BIT # BIT # BIT # BIT # BIT # BIT # BIT -> BYTE
        zero-byte : -> BYTE
    end

  imports
    Bits

  equations
    [01]  zero-byte = byte(bit0,bit0,bit0,bit0,bit0,bit0,bit0,bit0)

end Bytes
```

7.4.1.2 Symbols

The four basic data values that are transported around the network are the symbols *0, 1, J* and *K*. The module *Booleans* is imported from the standard library.

```
data module Symbols
begin

  exports
    begin
      sorts
        SYMBOL
      functions
        0 :                        -> SYMBOL
        1 :                        -> SYMBOL
        J :                        -> SYMBOL
        K :                        -> SYMBOL
        eq : SYMBOL # SYMBOL -> BOOLEAN
    end
```

```
imports
  Booleans

equations
  [01]  eq(0,0) = true
  [02]  eq(0,1) = false
  [03]  eq(0,J) = false
  [04]  eq(0,K) = false

  [05]  eq(1,0) = false
  [06]  eq(1,1) = true
  [07]  eq(1,J) = false
  [08]  eq(1,K) = false

  [09]  eq(J,0) = false
  [10]  eq(J,1) = false
  [11]  eq(J,J) = true
  [12]  eq(J,K) = false

  [13]  eq(K,0) = false
  [14]  eq(K,1) = false
  [15]  eq(K,J) = false
  [16]  eq(K,K) = true

end Symbols
```

7.4.1.3 Octets

While a byte is a collection of eight bits, an octet is a collection of eight symbols. Bytes are used for the communication with the environment, that is a higher OSI level, while octets are used for communication within the network. A byte can be interpreted as an octet in a straightforward way and an octet can be interpreted as a byte by interpreting J as a binary one and K as a binary zero.

```
data module Octets
begin

  exports
    begin
      sorts
        OCTET
      functions
        octet : SYMBOL # SYMBOL # SYMBOL # SYMBOL
                   # SYMBOL # SYMBOL # SYMBOL # SYMBOL -> OCTET
        octet : BYTE             -> OCTET
        byte  : OCTET            -> BYTE
        eq    : OCTET # OCTET -> BOOLEAN
    end

  imports
    Bits, Booleans, Bytes, Symbols

  functions
    symbol : BIT    -> SYMBOL
    bit    : SYMBOL -> BIT
```

```
variables
  b8, b7, b6, b5, b4, b3, b2, b1 : -> BIT
  s8, s7, s6, s5, s4, s3, s2, s1 : -> SYMBOL
  t8, t7, t6, t5, t4, t3, t2, t1 : -> SYMBOL

equations
  [01]  symbol(bit0) = 0
  [02]  symbol(bit1) = 1

  [03]  bit(0) = bit0
  [04]  bit(1) = bit1
  [05]  bit(J) = bit1
  [06]  bit(K) = bit0

  [07]  octet(byte(b8,b7,b6,b5,b4,b3,b2,b1)) =
           octet(symbol(b8),symbol(b7),symbol(b6),symbol(b5),
           symbol(b4),symbol(b3),symbol(b2),symbol(b1))

  [08]  eq(octet(s8,s7,s6,s5,s4,s3,s2,s1),
                    octet(t8,t7,t6,t5,t4,t3,t2,t1)) =
           and(eq(s8,t8), and(eq(s7,t7), and(eq(s6,t6),and(eq(s5,t5),
           and(eq(s4,t4), and(eq(s3,t3), and(eq(s2,t2), eq(s1,t1)))))))))

  [09]  byte(octet(s8,s7,s6,s5,s4,s3,s2,s1)) =
           byte(bit(s8),bit(s7),bit(s6),bit(s5),
                bit(s4),bit(s3),bit(s2),bit(s1))

end Octets
```

7.4.1.4 Fields

In this module some octets with a special meaning are defined. They are used to mark the fields in a message frame.

```
data module Fields
begin

  exports
    begin
      functions
        SD   : -> OCTET      -- Starting Delimiter
        ED   : -> OCTET      -- Ending Delimiter
        DONE : -> OCTET      -- transmission done
        IDLE : -> OCTET      -- a default octet
    end

  imports
    Octets, Symbols

  equations
    [01]  SD   = octet(J,K,0,J,K,0,0,0)
    [02]  ED   = octet(J,K,1,J,K,1,0,0)
    [03]  DONE = octet(J,K,1,J,K,0,0,0)
    [04]  IDLE = octet(0,0,0,0,0,0,0,0)

end Fields
```

7.4.1.5 SDU

A Service Data Unit (SDU) consists of a sequence of bytes. The library module Queues is used to represent such sequences.

```
data module SDU
begin

  imports
    Queues
      {Queue-parameter bound by
         [Q-ELEMENT -> BYTE,
           default-q-element -> zero-byte] to Bytes
       renamed by [QUEUE -> SDU]}

end SDU
```

7.4.1.6 Port Names

The actual number of stations and the order in which they are linked to each other is a parameter of the system. Every element of sort *PORT* determines a station. The function *next* defines the order in which the stations are connected. One of the stations has the monitor function assigned to it. This is the station related to the *monitor* port. Using the equality predicate on ports, we define the predicate *is-monitor*, which can be used to determine whether some given station is the monitor. The function *port-id* gives the octet which represents the port, while the function *port* determines the port that has a given octet as id.

```
data module PortNames
begin

  parameters
    Ports
      begin
        sorts
          PORT
        functions
          next    : PORT           -> PORT
          monitor :                -> PORT
          port-id : PORT           -> OCTET
          port    : OCTET          -> PORT
          eq      : PORT # PORT -> BOOLEAN
      end Ports

  exports
    begin
      functions
        is-monitor : PORT -> BOOLEAN
    end

  imports
    Booleans, Octets

  variables
    p : -> PORT
```

```
    equations
      [01]  is-monitor(p) = eq(p, monitor)

end PortNames
```

7.4.1.7 Utilities

In this module a number of special functions is defined, which deal with the manipulation of fields in a message frame. The Frame Status field (FS) is set by the sender of a frame using the *set-fs* function. If the receiver has read the frame, this will be acknowledged by applying the *ack-fs* function to the Frame Status octet.

The *is-token* function checks whether or not the access control field of a frame indicates that this frame is a token. The bit in the octet that determines this, can be set to any value using the *set-token* function. This token bit is a *0* in a token and a *1* in a frame.

```
    data module Utilities
    begin

      exports
        begin
          functions
            ack-fs     : OCTET              -> OCTET
            set-fs     : OCTET              -> OCTET
            is-token   : OCTET              -> BOOLEAN
            set-token  : OCTET # SYMBOL -> OCTET
        end

      imports
        Bits, Booleans, Bytes, Fields, PortNames, SDU

      variables
        symb, s8, s7, s6, s5, s4, s3, s2, s1 : -> SYMBOL

      equations
        [01]  ack-fs(octet(s8,s7,s6,s5,s4,s3,s2,s1)) =
                 octet(1,1,s6,s5,1,1,s2,s1)
        [02]  set-fs(octet(s8,s7,s6,s5,s4,s3,s2,s1)) =
                 octet(0,0,s6,s5,0,0,s2,s1)
        [03]  is-token(octet(s8,s7,s6,s5,s4,s3,s2,s1)) =
                 eq(s5,0)
        [04]  set-token(octet(s8,s7,s6,s5,s4,s3,s2,s1),symb) =
                 octet(s8,s7,s6,symb,s4,s3,s2,s1)

    end Utilities
```

7.4.2 PROCESS SPECIFICATION

Before giving the process definitions we give an overview of the architecture of the system with respect to the communication actions (see Figure 7.5). Every cluster consists of the ring interface proper and a buffer, which buffers an incoming SDU from a *request*. The ring interface can check if there is a message to send by using *pdu-queued*. If this is the case, the data is read one octet at a time by using *buf-req*. The *confirmation* is to indicate that the message has been sent successfully. Arrival of a message is signaled by *indication*.

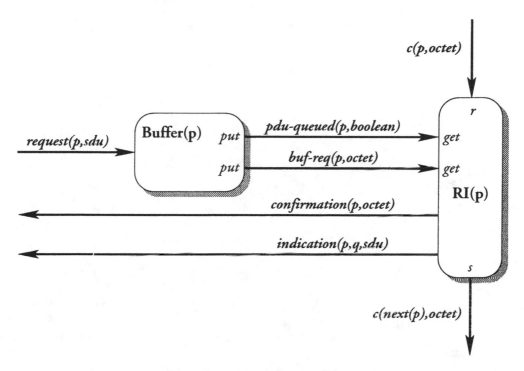

Figure 7.5   Communication ports

7.4.2.1 Ports

In the following module all atomic actions of the protocol and the communications in which they take part are listed. The communications are synchronous, which means that both partners in a communication must offer the possibility to communicate in order to let the communication take place.

```
process module Ports
begin

   exports
      begin

         atoms
            r : PORT # OCTET     -- read an octet from a port
            s : PORT # OCTET     -- write an octet into a port
            c : PORT # OCTET     -- communicate an octet on a port

            get-pdu-queued : PORT # BOOLEAN    -- is a PDU available?
            put-pdu-queued : PORT # BOOLEAN    -- tell if a PDU is available
            pdu-queued     : PORT # BOOLEAN    -- availability of a PDU
```

```
            get-buf-req : PORT # OCTET    -- get data from the buffer
            put-buf-req : PORT # OCTET    -- send data to the ring interface
            buf-req     : PORT # OCTET    -- octet from buffer to RI

            confirmation : PORT # OCTET          -- confirm transmission
            indication   : PORT # PORT # SDU     -- forward received data
            request      : PORT # PORT # SDU     -- accept data for sending

        end

    imports
      Utilities

    communications
      r(p,d) | s(p,d) = c(p,d)
        for p in PORT, d in OCTET
      get-pdu-queued(p,b) | put-pdu-queued(p,b) = pdu-queued(p,b)
        for p in PORT, b in BOOLEAN
      get-buf-req(p,d) | put-buf-req(p,d) = buf-req(p,d)
        for p in PORT, d in OCTET

   end Ports
```

7.4.2.2 Frame Reception

The process *RX-Frame* is invoked when a data frame is signalled by the ring-interface. The octet that is passed as the second argument is the first octet of the incoming frame following the starting delimiter. This is the access control octet, with the token bit set to 'data frame'. The first action is to write this octet unaltered onto the ring.

The next octet is then being read, which contains the destination address. If this address refers to the station's own address, the following octets are copied, otherwise the rest of the frame is simply repeated. Both activities continue until an ending delimiter is read. The difference between copying and repeating a frame is that copied frames are also passed on to the station by using the indication action. A copy ends in setting the acknowledgement bit in the frame status field.

```
    process module Frame-Reception
    begin

      exports
        begin
          processes
            RX-FRAME : PORT # OCTET
        end

      imports
        Ports, Utilities

      processes
        COPY   : PORT # SDU
        REPEAT : PORT
```

```
variables
  p      : -> PORT
  datum  : -> OCTET
  sdu    : -> SDU

definitions
  RX-FRAME(p,datum) =
      s(next(p),datum)
    . sum(d in OCTET,  r(p,d)
    . s(next(p),d)
    . (  [eq(port-id(p),d) = true] -> COPY(p,empty-queue)
      + [eq(port-id(p),d) = false] -> REPEAT(p)))

  COPY(p,sdu) =
      sum(d in OCTET,  r(p,d)
    . s(next(p),d)
    . (  [eq(d,ED) = true]
            ->   indication(p,port(octet(serve(sdu))),dequeue(sdu))
               . sum(fs in OCTET,  r(p,fs)
               . s(next(p),ack-fs(fs)))
      + [eq(d,ED) = false]
            -> COPY(p,enqueue(byte(d),sdu))))

  REPEAT(p) =
      sum(d in OCTET,  r(p,d)
    . s(next(p),d)
    . (  [eq(d,ED) = true]
            -> sum(fs in OCTET,  r(p,fs)  . s(next(p),fs))
      + [eq(d,ED) = false]
            -> REPEAT(p)))

end Frame-Reception
```

7.4.2.3 Token Transmission

The process *TX-TOKEN* generates a token on the selected port. This is done when the token ring is started up and whenever the token must be restored after a data transmission. As pointed out above, a token consists of a starting delimiter, followed by an access control octet having the token symbol set to *0*, followed by an ending delimiter.

```
process module  Token-Transmission
begin

  exports
    begin
      processes
        TX-TOKEN : PORT
    end

  imports
    Ports, Utilities

  variables
    p : -> PORT
```

```
definitions
  TX-TOKEN(p)  =
      s(next(p),SD)
    . s(next(p),set-token(IDLE,0))
    . s(next(p),ED)
```

end Token-Transmission

7.4.2.4 Frame Transmission

Every time the token passes a ring-interface, the process *TX-FRAME* is activated to decide whether the interface has to seize the token or to simply send it to the next ring-interface downstream. The octet that is passed as the second argument of *TX-FRAME* is the first octet of the incoming frame following the starting delimiter. This is the access control octet, with the token bit set to 'token frame'.

Whether the station has something to send or not is signalled by a *pdu-queued* action. If there is nothing to send, the token frame is simply repeated. Otherwise, the token is captured and replaced by a data frame.

First the token bit in the access control field is set to indicate that a data frame is being transmitted. After this, the ending delimiter octet is removed from the ring and the actual data octets are sent. This is done in parallel with the removal of the octets after they have propagated around the ring. The last octet in the stripped frame contains the frame status as set by the receiver. This octet is returned to our station with a *confirmation* action as an acknowledgement upon completion of the transmission.

The data octets are obtained from the buffer with the *get-buf-req* action. After all data octets have been sent, the token is regenerated.

```
process module  Frame-Transmission
begin

  exports
    begin
      processes
        TX-FRAME : PORT # OCTET
    end

  imports
    Ports, Token-Transmission, Utilities

  processes
    PDU      : PORT
    TX-DATA  : PORT
    STRIP    : PORT

  variables
    p  : -> PORT
    ac : -> OCTET
```

```
definitions
  TX-FRAME(p,ac) =
      get-pdu-queued(p,true).
            s(next(p),set-token(ac,1))
            . r(p,ED)
            . (TX-DATA(p) . TX-TOKEN(p) || r(p,SD) . STRIP(p))
      + get-pdu-queued(p,false).
            s(next(p),ac) . r(p,ED) . s(next(p),ED)


  TX-DATA(p) =
      sum(b in OCTET, get-buf-req(p,b)
    . s(next(p),b)
    . (   [eq(b,ED) = true]
            ->   s(next(p),set-fs(IDLE))
      + [eq(b,ED) = false]
            ->   TX-DATA(p)))


  STRIP(p) =
      sum(b in OCTET, r(p,b)
    . (   [eq(b,ED) = true]
            -> sum(fs in OCTET, r(p,fs) . confirmation(p,DONE))
      + [eq(b,ED) = false]
            -> STRIP(p)))


end Frame-Transmission
```

7.4.2.5 Ring Interfaces

The process *RI* is responsible for handling frames or tokens passing by. This process gets started when a starting delimiter is detected on the ring. Depending on whether the next field, the access control octet, signals a token or a frame, control is given to *TX-FRAME* or *RX-FRAME*.

```
process module Ring-Interfaces
begin

  exports
    begin
      processes
        RI : PORT
    end

  imports
    Frame-Reception, Frame-Transmission, Ports, Utilities

  variables
    p : -> PORT

  definitions
    RI(p) =
        r(p,SD)
      . s(next(p),SD)
      . sum(d in OCTET, r(p,d)
      . (   [is-token(d) = true] -> TX-FRAME(p,d) . RI(p)
        + [is-token(d) = false] -> RX-FRAME(p,d) . RI(p)))

end Ring-Interfaces
```

7.4.2.6 Buffers

A *Buffer* takes care of the incoming data via the *request* action. The first argument of this request is the station number and the second is the addressee. The buffer can hold one SDU and transmits it one octet at a time to the ring interface. Such a transmission starts by sending the port ids of the sender and receiver and ends by sending an ending delimiter.

The action *put-pdu-queued* signals whether data is available.

```
process module Buffer
begin

   exports
     begin
       processes
         Buffer : PORT
     end

   imports
     SDU, Ports, Utilities

   processes
     Buffer : PORT # SDU
     Buffer : PORT # PORT # SDU

   variables
     p,q  : -> PORT
     b    : -> BYTE
     sdu  : -> SDU

   definitions
     Buffer(p) =
         sum(sdu in SDU, sum(q in PORT,
                                 request(p,q,sdu) . Buffer(p,q,sdu)))
       + put-pdu-queued(p,false) . Buffer(p)
     Buffer(p,q,sdu) =
           put-buf-req(p,port-id(q))
         . put-buf-req(p,port-id(p))
         . Buffer(p,sdu)
       + put-pdu-queued(p,true) . Buffer(p,q,sdu)
     Buffer(p,sdu) =
           [eq(length(sdu),zero) = true]
                 -> put-buf-req(p,ED) . Buffer(p)
       + [eq(length(sdu),zero) = false]
                 ->    put-buf-req(p,octet(serve(sdu)))
                     . Buffer(p,dequeue(sdu))

end Buffer
```

7.4.2.7 Token Ring

This is the process module containing the main process *TokenRing*. The process *TokenRing* starts by initializing the ring network and then gets the ball rolling by generating a token on the monitor station. As mentioned above, no ring maintenance responsibilities are assigned to the monitor station in this specification. Thus, after having generated the first token, the monitor station will behave like all the other stations on the ring.

When the token is on the ring all stations and ring-interfaces are started up in parallel.

```
process module  TokenRing
begin

   exports
     begin
       processes
         TOKENRING
     end

   imports
     Ports, Ring-Interfaces, Buffer, Token-Transmission, Utilities

   processes
     CLUSTER  : PORT
     KICK-OFF : PORT

   sets of atoms
     C = { r(p,d), s(p,d) | p in PORT, d in OCTET }
     H =  { get-pdu-queued(p,b), put-pdu-queued(p,b) |
                              p in PORT, b in BOOLEAN }
        + { get-buf-req(p,b), put-buf-req(p,b) | p in PORT, b in OCTET }

   variables
     p : -> PORT

   definitions
     TOKENRING  = encaps(C, merge(p in PORT, CLUSTER(p)))

     CLUSTER(p) = (  [is-monitor(p) = true]
                         -> TX-TOKEN(p) . KICK-OFF(p)
                   + [is-monitor(p) = false]
                         -> KICK-OFF(p))

     KICK-OFF(p) = encaps(H, RI(p) || Buffer(p))

end TokenRing
```

7.5 SUMMARY

This work is a first step towards modelling the structure of a token ring network for a real system, namely IEEE 802.5. Although we made some abstractions and interpretations, it was made plausible that it is possible to do this with the specification formalism PSF.

By using an FDT, we obtained a specification of the token ring network in a modular way and we separated data types from the behaviour of the processes. This helps to get a deeper understanding of the overall function of such a network. As a result of having a specification, a formal verification of the correctness of the protocol comes into grasp.

We claim that all aspects of the token ring protocol which were not covered in this specification can be added easily, except for those dealing with time dependent operation. So it is possible to incorporate priority operation, broadcasting and ring maintenance by a monitor station in the specification. Real-time behaviour however, cannot be expressed in PSF.

7.6   BIBLIOGRAPHICAL NOTES

This chapter is based on [JM89].

Another FDT used for the specification of communication protocols is LOTOS [ISO89], which has been used to specify parts of the OSI standard (see [ISO88]).

IEEE has included a ring standard in Std. 802.5 [IEEE85b]. It has been adopted by ANSI as American National Standard, by NBS as a government standard and by ISO as international standard defined in ISO 8802.5.

A possible extension of ACP which deals with the incorporation of time is studied in [BB89].

APPENDIX A
THE PSF LIBRARY

A.1 INTRODUCTION

The specifications in this book make use of a collection of general modules which are collected in the PSF library. Chapter 2 contains a brief description of the data types defined in the library.

A.2 THE LIBRARY

A.2.1 BOOLEANS

```
data module Booleans
begin

  exports
    begin
      sorts
        BOOLEAN
      functions
        true : -> BOOLEAN
        false : -> BOOLEAN
        eq : BOOLEAN # BOOLEAN -> BOOLEAN
        not : BOOLEAN -> BOOLEAN
        and : BOOLEAN # BOOLEAN -> BOOLEAN
        or : BOOLEAN # BOOLEAN -> BOOLEAN
        xor : BOOLEAN # BOOLEAN -> BOOLEAN
    end
```

```
variables
  b : -> BOOLEAN

equations
  [01] eq(true, true) = true
  [02] eq(true, false) = false
  [03] eq(false, true) = false
  [04] eq(false, false) = true
  [05] not(true) = false
  [06] not(false) = true
  [07] and(true, b) = b
  [08] and(false, b) = false
  [09] or(true, b) = true
  [10] or(false, b) = b
  [11] xor(b, b) = false
  [12] xor(true, false) = true
  [13] xor(false, true) = true


end Booleans
```

A.2.2   NATURALS

```
data module Naturals
begin

  exports
    begin
      sorts
        NATURAL
      functions
        zero : -> NATURAL
        s : NATURAL -> NATURAL
        eq : NATURAL # NATURAL -> BOOLEAN
        gte : NATURAL # NATURAL -> BOOLEAN
        gt : NATURAL # NATURAL -> BOOLEAN
        lte : NATURAL # NATURAL -> BOOLEAN
        lt : NATURAL # NATURAL -> BOOLEAN
        inc : NATURAL -> NATURAL
        dec : NATURAL -> NATURAL
        _+_ : NATURAL # NATURAL -> NATURAL
        _-_ : NATURAL # NATURAL -> NATURAL
        _*_ : NATURAL # NATURAL -> NATURAL
        mod : NATURAL # NATURAL -> NATURAL
        div : NATURAL # NATURAL -> NATURAL
    end

  imports
    Booleans

  variables
    n,m : -> NATURAL
```

```
equations
  [01] eq(zero, zero) = true
  [02] eq(zero, s(m)) = false
  [03] eq(s(n), zero) = false
  [04] eq(s(n), s(m)) = eq(n,m)

  [05] inc(n) = s(n)
  [06] dec(s(n)) = n
  [07] dec(zero) = zero

  [08] gte(n, zero) = true
  [09] gte(s(n), s(m)) = gte(n,m)
  [10] gte(zero, s(m)) = false
  [11] gt(n, m) = not(gte(m,n))
  [12] lt(n, m) = not(gte(n,m))
  [13] lte(n, m) = gte(m,n)

  [14] n + zero = n
  [15] n + s(m) = inc(n + m)
  [16] n - zero = n
  [17] n - s(m) = dec(n - m)
  [18] n * zero = zero
  [19] n * s(m) = n + (n * m)

  [20] div(zero, n) = zero
  [21] div(n, zero) = zero
  [22] div(n, m) = zero when lt(n, m) = true
  [23] div(n, s(m)) = inc(div(n - s(m), s(m)))
         when lt(n, s(m)) = false
  [24] mod(n, m) = n - (div(n, m) * m)

end Naturals
```

A.2.3   BITS

```
data module Bits
begin

  exports
    begin
      sorts
        BIT
      functions
        bit0 : -> BIT
        bit1 : -> BIT
        invert : BIT -> BIT
        unary : BIT -> NATURAL
        eq : BIT # BIT -> BOOLEAN
    end

  imports
    Naturals
```

```
equations
  [01] invert(bit0) = bit1
  [02] invert(bit1) = bit0
  [03] unary(bit0) = zero
  [04] unary(bit1) = s(zero)
  [05] eq(bit0, bit0) = true
  [06] eq(bit0, bit1) = false
  [07] eq(bit1, bit0) = false
  [08] eq(bit1, bit1) = true

end Bits
```

A.2.4   DATA

```
data module Data
begin

  parameters
    Data-parameter
      begin
        sorts
          DATA
        functions
          default-data : -> DATA
      end Data-parameter

end Data
```

A.2.5   QUEUES

```
data module Queues
begin

  parameters
    Queue-parameter
      begin
        sorts
          Q-ELEMENT
        functions
          default-q-element : -> Q-ELEMENT
      end Queue-parameter

  exports
    begin
      sorts
        QUEUE
      functions
        empty-queue : -> QUEUE
        enqueue : Q-ELEMENT # QUEUE -> QUEUE
        serve : QUEUE -> Q-ELEMENT
        dequeue : QUEUE -> QUEUE
        length : QUEUE -> NATURAL
    end
```

```
imports
  Naturals

functions
  _*_  :  Q-ELEMENT # QUEUE -> QUEUE

variables
  e,e' : -> Q-ELEMENT
  q : -> QUEUE

equations
  [01]  enqueue(e,q) = e * q
  [02]  serve(empty-queue) = default-q-element
  [03]  serve(e * empty-queue) = e
  [04]  serve(e * (e' * q)) = serve(e' * q)
  [05]  dequeue(empty-queue) = empty-queue
  [06]  dequeue(e * empty-queue) = empty-queue
  [07]  dequeue(e * (e' * q)) = e * dequeue(e' * q)
  [08]  length(empty-queue) = zero
  [09]  length(e * q) = s(length(q))

end Queues
```

A.2.6   TABLES

```
data module Tables
begin

  parameters
    Keys
      begin
        sorts
          KEY
        functions
          eq : KEY # KEY -> BOOLEAN
      end Keys,

    Items
      begin
        sorts
          ITEM
        functions
          default-item : -> ITEM
      end Items
```

```
exports
  begin
    sorts
      TABLE, ENTRY
    functions
      empty-table : -> TABLE
      insert : TABLE # ITEM # KEY -> TABLE
      retrieve : TABLE # KEY -> ITEM
      delete : TABLE # KEY -> TABLE
      in-table : TABLE # KEY -> BOOLEAN
      length : TABLE -> NATURAL
      entry : KEY # ITEM -> ENTRY
      _*_ : ENTRY # TABLE -> TABLE
  end

imports
  Naturals

variables
  k,k' : -> KEY
  i,i' : -> ITEM
  t : -> TABLE

equations
  [01] insert(empty-table,i,k) = entry(k,i) * empty-table
  [02] insert(entry(k,i') * t,i,k') = entry(k,i) * t
          when eq(k,k') = true
  [03] insert(entry(k,i') * t,i,k') = entry(k,i') * insert(t,i,k')
          when eq(k,k') = false
  [04] retrieve(empty-table,k) = default-item
  [05] retrieve(entry(k,i) * t,k') = i
          when eq(k,k') = true
  [06] retrieve(entry(k,i) * t,k') = retrieve(t,k')
          when eq(k,k') = false
  [07] delete(empty-table,k) = empty-table
  [08] delete(entry(k,i) * t,k') = t
          when eq(k,k') = true
  [09] delete(entry(k,i) * t,k') = entry(k,i) * delete(t,k')
          when eq(k,k') = false
  [10] in-table(empty-table,k) = false
  [11] in-table(entry(k,i) * t,k') = true
          when eq(k,k') = true
  [12] in-table(entry(k,i) * t,k') = in-table(t,k')
          when eq(k,k') = false
  [13] length(empty-table) = zero
  [14] length(entry(k,i) * t) = s(length(t))

end Tables
```

Appendix B
Syntax of PSF

B.1 Context-free Syntax

The grammar for PSF is defined with the use of the following abbreviations:

- [<N>] denotes an optional occurrence of <N>;
- <N>+ denotes one or more occurrences of <N>;
- { <N> t }+ denotes one or more occurrences of <N> separated by terminal symbol t.

```
<specification>        ::= <module>+
<module>               ::= <data-module> | <process-module>
<data-module>          ::= "data" "module" <module-ident>
                           "begin"
                               [ <d-parameters> ]
                               [ <d-exports> ]
                               [ <imports> ]
                               [ <sorts> ]
                               [ <functions> ]
                               [ <d-variables> ]
                               [ <equations> ]
                           "end" <module-ident>
<d-parameters>         ::= "parameters" { <d-parameter> "," }+
<d-parameter>          ::= <parameter-ident>
                           "begin"
                               [ <sorts> ]
                               [ <functions> ]
                           "end" <parameter-ident>
<d-exports>            ::= "exports"
                           "begin"
                               [ <sorts> ]
                               [ <functions> ]
                           "end"
<imports>              ::= "imports" { <module-expression> "," }+
```

185

```
<module-expression>        ::= <module-ident> [ "{" <modifier> "}" ]
<modifier>                 ::= <renamed> [ <bindings> ] |
                               <bindings> [ <renamed> ]
<renamed>                  ::= "renamed" "by" <renamings>
<renamings>                ::= "[" { <renaming> "," }+ "]"
<renaming>                 ::= <ident-or-operator> "->" <ident-or-operator>
<ident-or-operator>        ::= <ident> |
                               "_" <operator> "_" |
                               <operator> "_"
<bindings>                 ::= ( <parameter-ident>
                                  "bound" [ "by" <renamings> ]
                                  "to" <module-ident> )+
<sorts>                    ::= "sorts" { <sort-ident> "," }+
<functions>               ::= "functions" <function>+
<function>                ::= <fun-ident> ":" [ <input-type> ]
                                               "->" <sort-ident> |
                               <operator> "_" ":" <sort-ident>
                                               "->" <sort-ident> |
                               "_" <operator> "_" ":"
                                  <sort-ident> "#" <sort-ident>
                                               "->" <sort-ident>
<input-type>              ::= { <sort-ident> "#" }+
<d-variables>             ::= "variables" <d-variable-list>
<d-variable-list>         ::= ( <var-ident-list> ":" "->" <sort-ident> )+
<var-ident-list>          ::= { <var-ident> "," }+
<equations>               ::= "equations" <cond-equation>+
<cond-equation>           ::= <tag> <equation> |
                               <tag> <equation-list> <implies> <equation> |
                               <tag> <equation> "when" <equation-list>
<tag>                     ::= "[" <tag-ident> "]"
<equation-list>           ::= { <equation> "," }+
<equation>                ::= <term> "=" <term>
<term>                    ::= <term-primary> |
                               <term> <operator> <term-primary>
<term-primary>            ::= <fun-ident> [ "(" <term-list> ")" ] |
                               <var-ident> |
                               "(" <term> ")" |
                               <operator> <term-primary>
<term-list>               ::= { <term> "," }+
<process-module>          ::= "process" "module" <module-ident>
                               "begin"
                                   [ <p-parameters> ]
                                   [ <p-exports> ]
                                   [ <imports> ]
                                   [ <atoms> ]
                                   [ <processes> ]
                                   [ <sets> ]
                                   [ <communications> ]
                                   [ <p-variables> ]
                                   [ <definitions> ]
                               "end" <module-ident>
<p-parameters>            ::= "parameters" { <p-parameter> "," }+
<p-parameter>             ::= <parameter-ident>
                               "begin"
                                   [ <sorts> ]
                                   [ <functions> ]
```

```
                                          [ <atoms> ]
                                          [ <processes> ]
                                          [ <sets-param> ]
                                       "end" <parameter-ident>
      <p-exports>                   ::= "exports"
                                       "begin"
                                          [ <atoms> ]
                                          [ <processes> ]
                                          [ <sets> ]
                                       "end"
      <atoms>                       ::= "atoms" <atom-decl-list>+
      <atom-decl-list>              ::= { <atom-ident> "," }+ [ ":" <input-type> ]
      <processes>                   ::= "processes" <process-decl-list>+
      <process-decl-list>           ::= { <process-ident> "," }+ [ ":" <input-type> ]
      <sets-param>                  ::= "sets" ( <of-sort-or-atoms> <set-ident>+ )+
      <sets>                        ::= "sets" ( <of-sort-or-atoms> <set-decl>+ )+
      <of-sort-or-atoms>            ::= "of" <sort-ident> | "of" "atoms"
      <set-decl>                    ::= <set-ident> "=" <set-exp>
      <set-exp>                     ::= <set-tertiary> |
                                        <set-exp> "+" <set-tertiary>
      <set-tertiary>                ::= <set-secondary> |
                                        <set-primary> "\" <set-secondary>
      <set-secondary>               ::= <set-primary> |
                                        <set-secondary> "." <set-primary>
      <set-primary>                 ::= <sort-or-set-ident> |
                                        "(" <set-exp> ")" |
                                        "{" [ <term-list> [ "|" <placeholders> ]] "}"
      <sort-or-set-ident>           ::= <sort-ident> | <set-ident>
      <placeholders>                ::= { <placeholder> "," }+
      <placeholder>                 ::= <var-ident> "in" <sort-or-set-ident>
      <p-variables>                 ::= "variables" <p-variable-list>
      <p-variable-list>             ::= ( <var-ident-list> ":"
                                            "->" <sort-or-set-ident> )+
      <communications>              ::= "communications" <communication>+
      <communication>               ::= <atom> "|" <atom> "=" <atom>
                                            [ "for" <placeholders> ]
      <atom>                        ::= <atom-ident> [ "(" <term-list> ")" ]
      <definitions>                 ::= "definitions" <definition>+
      <definition>                  ::= <simple-process> "=" <process>
      <simple-process>              ::= <process-ident> [ "(" <term-list> ")" ]
      <process>                     ::= <process-tertiary> |
                                        <process> "+" <process-tertiary>
      <process-tertiary>            ::= <process-secondary> |
                                        <process-primary> "||" <process-secondary>
      <process-secondary>           ::= <process-primary> |
                                        <process-secondary> "." <process-primary>
      <process-primary>             ::= "skip" |
                                        "delta" |
                                        <simple-process> |
                                        "(" <process> ")" |
                                        "sum" "(" placeholder "," <process> ")" |
                                        "merge" "(" placeholder "," <process> ")" |
                                        "hide" "(" <sort-or-set-ident> ","
                                                                <process> ")" |
                                        "encaps" "(" <sort-or-set-ident> ","
                                                                <process> ")"
```

```
<module-ident>          ::= <ident>
<parameter-ident>       ::= <ident>
<sort-ident>            ::= <ident>
<fun-ident>             ::= <ident>
<var-ident>             ::= <ident>
<tag-ident>             ::= <ident>
<atom-ident>            ::= <ident>
<process-ident>         ::= <ident>
<set-ident>             ::= <ident>
```

B.2 LEXICAL SYNTAX

Layout characters:
  space, horizontal tabulation, carriage return, line feed, form feed

Comments:
  Comments begin with two hyphens and end with either an end of line or another pair of hyphens. The character immediately preceding a comment (if there is one) must be a layout character.

Identifiers:
  Identifiers consist of a non-empty sequence of letters, digits or single-quote characters, possibly with embedded hyphens.
  - examples: i, me, type-writer, prime', 'quotation', double--hyphen
  - non-examples: -x, -, x-

Operators:
  Operators are denoted by a non-empty sequence of operator symbols or an identifier surrounded by dots. Possible operator symbols are:
  ! @ $ % ^ & + - * ; ? ~ / | \
  - examples: &&, -?-, .push., %^@$, .'id., .greater-than.
  - non-examples: >=, push, .@., @a

Implication symbol:
  An implication symbol consists of two or more equal signs (=), optionally followed by a greater-than sign (>).
  - examples: ==, ==>, ==================

Reserved keywords:

atoms	exports	processes
begin	for	renamed
bound	functions	sets
by	hide	skip
communications	imports	sorts
data	in	sum
definitions	merge	to
delta	module	variables
encaps	of	when
end	parameters	
equations	process	

REFERENCES

[Bae90]   J.C.M. Baeten (ed), *Applications of Process Algebra*, Cambridge University Press, 1990.

[BB87]   T. Bolognesi & E. Brinksma, *Introduction to the ISO Specification Language LOTOS*, Computer Networks and ISDN Systems 14, pp. 25-59, Elsevier Science Publishers, 1987.

[BB89]   J.C.M. Baeten & J.A. Bergstra, *Real time process algebra* Journal of Formal Aspects of Computing Science, 3(2), pp. 142-188, 1991.

[BHK89]   J.A. Bergstra, J. Heering & P. Klint, *The algebraic specification formalism ASF*, in: *Algebraic specification*, J.A. Bergstra, J. Heering & P. Klint (eds.), pp. 1-66, ACM Press Frontier Series, Addison-Wesley 1989.

[BK84]   J.A. Bergstra & J.W. Klop, *Process algebra for synchronous communication*, Information & Control 60, pp. 109-137, 1984.

[Bru91a]   J.J. Brunekreef, *A Formal Specification of three Sliding Window Protocols (revised version)*, report P9102b, University of Amsterdam, 1991

[Bru91b]   J.J. Brunekreef, *A Formal Specification of the Amoeba Transaction Protocol*, report P9108, University of Amsterdam, 1991.

[Bru91c]   J.J. Brunekreef, *A Formal Specification of Two Simple Protocols for Local Area Networks*, report P9109, University of Amsterdam, 1991.

[BW90]   J.C.M. Baeten & W.P. Weijland, *Process Algebra*, Cambridge Tracts in Theoretical Computer Science 18, Cambridge University Press, 1990.

[CPS89]   R. Cleaveland, J. Parrow & B. Steffen, *The Concurrency Workbench*, in: Proceedings of the Workshop on Automatic Verification Methods for Finite-State Systems, (J. Sifakis, ed.), LNCS 407, pp. 24-37, Springer Verlag, 1989.

[Dik89]   C.H.S. Dik, *A Fast Implementation of the Algebraic Specification Formalism*, Master's Thesis, University of Amsterdam, 1989.

[Eij91]   P. van Eijk, *Tools for LOTOS, a Lotosphere overview*, in: Proc. IFIP TC6/WG6.1, FORTE '91, Sydney, (G.A. Rose & K.R. Parker, eds.), North-Holland, 1991.

[EM85]   H. Ehrig & B. Mahr, *Fundamentals of Algebraic Specifications, Vol. I, Equations and Initial Semantics*, Springer-Verlag, 1985.

[FM91]   J.C. Fernandez & L. Mounier, *A Tool Set for deciding Behavioral Equivalences*, in: Proceedings CONCUR '91, Amsterdam, (J.C.M. Baeten & J.F. Groote, eds.), LNCS 527, pp. 23-42, Springer Verlag, 1991.

[FJ92]   L.M.G. Feijs, H.B.M. Jonkers, *Formal specification and design*, Cambridge Tracts in Theoretical Computer Science 35, Cambridge University Press, 1992.

[GM85]   J.A. Goguen & J. Meseguer, *Initiality, induction and computability*, in: Algebraic Methods in Semantics (M. Nivat & J.C. Reynolds eds.), pp. 460-541, Cambridge University Press, 1985.

[GP90]   J.F. Groote & A. Ponse, *The syntax and semantics of μCRL*, Report CS-R9076, CWI, Amsterdam, 1990.

[Gro87]   R.A. Groenveld, *Verification of a Sliding Window Protocol by means of Process Algebra*, report P8701, University of Amsterdam, 1987.

[Gro91]   J.F. Groote, *Process Algebra and Structured Operational Semantics*, Ph.D. Thesis, University of Amsterdam, 1991.

[GV89]   R.J. van Glabbeek & F.W. Vaandrager, *Modular specifications in process algebra- with curious queues*, in: Algebraic Methods: Theory, Tools and Applications (M. Wirsing & J.A. Bergstra, eds.), LNCS 394, Springer Verlag, pp. 465-506, 1989.

[GV90]   J.F. Groote & F.W. Vaandrager, *An efficient algorithm for branching bisimulation and stuttering equivalence*, in: Proc. 17th ICALP, Warwick, (M.S. Paterson, ed.) LNCS 443, pp. 626-638, Springer Verlag, 1990.

[HM85]   M. Hennessy & R. Milner, *Algebraic Laws for Nondeterminism and Concurrency*, in: Journal of the ACM, vol. 32, nr. 1, pp. 137-161, 1985.

[Hoa85]   C.A.R. Hoare, *Communicating Sequential Processes*, Prentice-Hall, 1985.

[HS88]   J. Hershall & S. Shaw, *OSI explained, end-to-end computer communication standards*, Ellis Horwood Limited, 1988.

[IEEE85a]   ANSI/IEEE, *Logical Link Control*, standard 802.2, IEEE, New York, 1985.

[IEEE85b]   ANSI/IEEE, *Token Ring Access Method*, standard 802.5, IEEE, New York, 1985.

[IEEE85c]   ANSI/IEEE, *Carrier Sense Multiple Access with Collision Detection*, standard 802.3, IEEE, New York, 1985.

[ISO88]   ISO, ISO/IEC JTC1/SC6 N4870, Formal description of ISO 8072 in LOTOS (PDTR 10023).

[ISO89]   International Organization for Standardization, *IS 8807, Information processing systems - Open systems interconnection - LOTOS - A Formal Description Technique Based on the Temporal Ordering of Observational Behaviour*, ISO 1989.

[JM89]   H. Jacobsson & S. Mauw, *A token ring network in PSF$_d$*, Report P8914, Programming Research Group, University of Amsterdam, 1989.

[Kap87]   S. Kaplan, *A Compiler for Conditional Term Rewriting Systems*, in: Rewriting Techniques and Applications, (P. Lescanne, ed.), LNCS 256, pp. 25-41, Springer Verlag, 1987.

[KM90]   C.P.J. Koymans & J.C. Mulder, *A modular approach to protocol verification using process algebra*, in [Bae90], 1990.

[Kor92]   H.P. Korver, *Computing distinguishing formulas for branching bisimulation*, in: Proc. Third Workshop on Computer Aided Verification, Aalborg, (K.G. Larsen & A. Skou, eds.), LNCS 575, pp. 13-23, Springer Verlag, 1992.

[Lin92]   H. Lin, *PAM: A Process Algebra Manipulator*, in: Proc. Third Workshop on Computer Aided Verification, Aalborg, (K.G. Larsen & A. Skou, eds.), LNCS 575, pp. 136-146, Springer Verlag, 1992.

[Mau90]   S. Mauw, *Process algebra as a tool for the specification and verification of CIM-architectures*, in [Bae90], 1990.

[Mau91]   S. Mauw, *PSF, A process Specification Formalism*, Ph.D. Thesis, Programming Research Group, University of Amsterdam, 1991.

[Mid86]   A. Middeldorp, *Specification of a sliding window protocol within the framework of process algebra*, report FVI 86-19, University of Amsterdam, 1986.

[Mil89]   R. Milner, *Communication and Concurrency*, Prentice Hall, 1989.

[MM90]   S. Mauw & Gy. Max, *A formal specification of the ethernet protocol*, Report P9007, Programming Research Group, University of Amsterdam, 1990.

[Mul85]   S.J. Mullender, *Principles of Distributed Operating System Design*, Ph.D. Thesis, Free University, Amsterdam, 1985.

[Mul90]   J.C. Mulder, *On the Amoeba protocol*, in [Bae90], 1990.

[MV89a]   S. Mauw & G.J. Veltink, *An introduction to PSF$_d$*, in: Proc. International Joint Conference on Theory and Practice of Software Development, TAPSOFT '89, (J. Díaz, F. Orejas, eds.) LNCS 352, vol. 2, pp. 272-285, Springer Verlag, 1989.

[MV89b]   S. Mauw & G.J. Veltink, *A Tool Interface Language for PSF*, Report P8912, Programming Research Group, University of Amsterdam, 1989.

[MV90]   S. Mauw & G.J. Veltink, *A process specification formalism*, Fundamenta Informaticae XIII (1990), pp. 85-139, IOS Press, 1990.

[MV92]   S. Mauw & G.J. Veltink, *A proof assistant for PSF*, in: Proc. Third
           Workshop on Computer Aided Verification, Aalborg, (K.G. Larsen & A.
           Skou, eds.), Aalborg 1991, LNCS 575, pp. 158-168, Springer Verlag, 1992.

[MW89]   S. Mauw & F. Wiedijk, *Specification of the Transit Node in PSF$_d$*, in:
           Algebraic Methods II: Theory, Tools and Applications (J.A. Bergstra &
           L.M.G. Feijs, eds), Springer LNCS 490, pp. 341-361, 1991.

[Par81]   D.M.R. Park, *Concurrency and automata on infinite sequences*, in: Proc.
           5th GI Conf. (P. Deussen, ed.), Springer LNCS 104, pp. 167-183, 1981.

[Plo82]   G.D. Plotkin, *An operational semantics for CSP*, in: Proc. Conf. Formal
           Description of Programming Concepts II, Garmisch 1982 (E. Bjørner, ed.),
           pp. 199-225, North-Holland, 1982.

[Pol92]   E.E. Polak, *An efficient implementation of branching bisimulation and
           distinguishing formulae*, report P9216, University of Amsterdam, 1992.

[Sch87]   M. Schwartz, *Telecommunication networks: protocols, modeling and
           analysis*, Addison-Wesley, 1987.

[SDL84]   *Functional Specification and Description Language (SDL)*, CCITT,
           Recommendation Z.100-Z.104, Geneva, 1984.

[Tan89]   A. S. Tanenbaum, *Computer Networks*, Prentice Hall, 1989.

[Vaa86]   F.W. Vaandrager, *Verification of two communication protocols by means
           of process algebra*, Report CS-R8606, Centre for Mathematics and
           Computer Science, Amsterdam, 1986.

[Vaa90]   F.W. Vaandrager, *Two simple protocols*, in [Bae90], 1990.

[VDM88]   *VDM specification language proto-standard*, draft, BSI IST/5/50,
           Document N-40, 1988.

[Vel90]   G.J. Veltink, *From PSF to TIL*, Report P9009, Programming Research
           Group, University of Amsterdam, 1990.

[Vel91]   G.J. Veltink, *XP, an experiment in modular specification*, in: Proc. IFIP
           TC6/WG6.1, FORTE '91, Sydney, (G.A. Rose & K.R. Parker, eds.), North-
           Holland, 1991.

[Ver91]   D. Vergamini, *Auto/Mauto Users' Manual*, INRIA Research Report 111,
           INRIA, 1991.

[VW92]   S.F.M. van Vlijmen & A. van Waveren, *An algebraic specification of a
           model factory*, Report P9209, Programming Research Group, University of
           Amsterdam, 1992.

[Wam92a]   J.J. van Wamel, *An algebraic verification of the concurrent alternating
           bit protocol*, Report P9205, University of Amsterdam, 1992.

[Wam92b]   J.J. van Wamel, *A study of a one bit sliding window protocol*, Report
           P9212, University of Amsterdam, 1992.

MODULE INDEX

SUBJECT INDEX

195